CUSTOMIZING YOUR
HARLEY-DAVIDSON

276·3303
ARLEN NESS NOW OPEN
MONDAYS
Arlen Ness

CUSTOMIZING YOUR HARLEY-DAVIDSON

PATRICK HOOK

ACKNOWLEDGMENTS

ABOVE LEFT: Jeff Duval, owner of Battistinis.
ABOVE RIGHT: Rick James, Nathan Roberts, and Steve Cox.

The Publisher and Author should like to thank Battistinis — particularly Peter Allcock — and Arlen Ness for the substantial assistance received, and Simon Clay for the excellent photography. Thanks also go to all those who supplied their bikes for photography.

SAFETY

Before starting to customize your Harley, consult all appropriate factory recommendations and
FOLLOW THE INSTRUCTIONS TO THE LETTER.
Customizing involves use of a variety of tools: at all times pay attention to safety considerations. Matters such as eye protection are vital, as are wearing gloves and keeping long hair secured away from moving machinery.
Inflammable materials should be dealt with as appropriate — and with great care — battery acids should not be ingested and fingers are best kept out of trip-hammers.

Some products used in customizing may be poisonous,
so don't lick your fingers when working with radioactive isotopes and certain synthetic oils.
All opinions expressed in this book are the Author's, and the Author and Publisher accept no responsibility for any work undertaken as a result of reading this book.
Any work performed by the reader is entirely at his own risk; if in doubt consult a local expert.
Remember that motorcycles have to adhere to international, national, and local safety and mechanical requirements and some of the parts mentioned in this book are suitable only for sports use.

Photograph page 1: Dave Stewart's Trike. See page 188..
Photograph page 2: Arlen Ness on Ness Stalgia. See pages 70-71.
Photograph page 3: Smoothness. See page 180.

This edition published in 1998 by
Thunder Bay Press
5880 Oberlin Drive, Suite 400
San Diego, California 92121
1-800-284-3580

http:/www.adms.web.com

Produced by
PRC Publishing Ltd,
Kiln House, 210 New Kings Road, London SW6 4NZ

ISBN 1 57145 136 6

Printed and bound in China

CONTENTS

INTRODUCTION

Before we look at why people choose to customize their Harley, let's just take a look at exactly what "customizing" means. The precise definition is to "personalize" — so for Harley enthusiasts it equates to taking a motorcycle and altering things to suit their individual requirements or tastes. Every component is entirely up to the owner — he may decide to build anything from a wild chop to a pocket rocket. There again, the owner may just want to make the bike fit himself better — the manufacturer doesn't usually know the individual characteristics of the rider who could be anywhere between five and seven feet tall. For some owners, however, the bike is just fine and dandy as it is, so nothing more than a custom paint job reflecting something personal may be wanted.

The real start of customizing as we know it was at the end of World War 2, when ex-military Harleys were sold off cheap at surplus depots. A lot of them were bought by servicemen returning from Europe or the Far East — men who wanted a taste of the freedom of the roads that a motorcycle could give. These war vets often wanted more performance than the overweight service models were able to provide — especially as the more expensive bikes of the time were the lighter, faster, English makes, such as Norton and Triumph.

The easiest and cheapest way to keep up with the quicker opposition was to remove as much weight as

ABOVE: Although it looks like a Harley-Davidson, this is in fact a "Big Dog" — a complete Harley look-alike built without using any factory parts.

RIGHT: The unmistakable lines of a Fatboy make it very popular with many riders, practical for everyday use, long distances and for street cruising. The Fatboy forms the basis of many customs from mild to wild.

MAURICE

possible: things like fenders, luggage racks, windshields, etc., got trashed. This was customizing for practical reasons, and was where the word "chop" comes from — it literally meant "chopped and dropped." Another expression used at the time was "bobbing," which has lived on to this day with names like "fatbob tanks," or "bobbed" fenders. A side effect of all this activity was that the bikes got to look leaner and meaner, which in turn led to modifications for purely aesthetic reasons.

Hollywood (of course) had its part to play in all this — films like *The Wild One* had a huge influence on the way bikes were perceived, both by the general public and by motorcyclists themselves. Furthermore, the media had found itself a universal "bad guy," an image used and abused to this day. Many of the riders themselves felt frustrated by the clean-cut ideals and attitudes of the 1950s and wanted a way to rebel. Now they had the opportunity and the perfect mechanism with which to express their rebellion. The new culture of the 1960s, together with the new affluence of the young, combined to produce a backdrop against which customizing for style reasons alone took off.

In 1969 the attitudes and longings of an entire generation were reflected with the most famous biker movie of all time — *Easy Rider.* It drew together music, freedom, peace and love — all the elements of 1960s' youth, and contrasted it with the bigotry and animosity of the redneck establishment. It spoke directly to the multitudes of people who had chosen to grow their hair long and "do their own thing." Most of them were only too aware of the 1950s' mentality still evident everywhere around them.

The various movies depicting bikers as bad guys rebeling against the system spawned the desire to build custom bikes wherever they were shown. In the early days there was a struggle to out-do the next guy with higher handlebars, longer exhausts, less brakes, smaller gas tanks and freakier paint jobs. Many of these bikes were totally impractical, and a lot were almost unrideable, sometimes ending up only for exhibition. Some bikes were all for show and didn't even have engine internals!

During this time the fledgling custom parts business boomed. There were many backstreet shops performing customizing work to keep up with the demand. Much of this work was at best second-rate, and the quality of many custom parts sold was often very poor. Thankfully, most of these have given way to the laws of economics and disappeared from whence they came. Gradually over the years the surviving pioneers of the custom bike business have evolved into the multi-million dollar industry we have now.

Since the start of the 1990s, the quality of custom bikes has changed considerably, led by a few of the top names in the business such as John Reed, Arlen Ness and Battistinis. These people have worked hard to prototype innovative products for the aftermarket. This means that a custom builder today has access to standards of design and manufacture that could only be dreamed about until recent times. They have set new standards for us all to emulate. These leading exponents of custom design are never satisfied and are forever trying to outdo themselves with better products.

One of the great leaps forward in the aftermarket industry has been the widespread use of CNC techniques. CNC is an acronym for "computer numerical control," a form of manufacture that has become more popular as the machinery has become available. The beauty of CNC is that very complicated components can be made to incredible standards of accuracy, time after time. This means that custom bike parts, which would have taken a skilled engineer hundreds of hours of intensive machining, are now produced under the supervision of a computer. Combined with the widespread use of forged billet aluminum, this has resulted in things like CNC cylinder heads and crankcases being offered for sale.

The vast choice of these high quality components means that we can build our projects to the same standards as the best showbikes around! The downside is that if we build our bikes using too many aftermarket parts, we run the risk of creating a bike that's not totally original. My opinion is that a good blend of custom parts mixed with home-made ones will result in a bike to be proud of; I see no point in busting a gut to make a part that you could easily purchase. However, if you want to save your money for another component, or if you simply want to prove a point, then go ahead — make anything you can.

RIGHT: Some people prefer touring bikes to customs. This bike could be used to tour long distances comfortably. Tourers are much less likely to be customized as added to for long-distance practicality. The sorts of modifications for a tourer include more luggage carrying capacity, better weather protection, and more comfortable seats and footboards. The engine could receive attention to boost low- and mid-range torque and the brakes could be upgraded, along with the suspension. Many touring riders like to add extra lights, both front and rear.

WHY HARLEYS?

Why are Harleys in particular the most popular subject of customizers the world over? There are lots of good reasons. For many it's because they won't look at any motorcycle that's not American. For some it's the whole of the Harley "lifestyle" thing; for others, it's because they love the unique sound and feel of the engine. Whatever the reason, Harleys remain the ultimate desire for most young riders and command a loyalty that other manufacturers can only dream of.

One of the major attractions for choosing a Harley for a custom project is that you can work on it without a university degree in rocket science. Most other modern bikes are much too complicated for a home mechanic to perform any major surgery on. Another feature is that Harleys can be worked on and upgraded a little at a time for years. This spreads the cost and effort over a long period, with parts often getting changed only when they're due for replacement anyway. If you end up building a really radical bike, you'll get the inevitable comments from jealous onlookers along the lines of "it's not really a Harley anymore is it?" If I had a dollar for every time I've heard that, I'd be a rich man. If the bike started out as a Harley, or if it's recognizable as something derived from the Milwaukee product, then that should be good enough for anyone with the wits to appreciate a class act.

Before we take a look at the many possible improvements that can be made to a Harley motor, we need to examine how it's constructed. The basic configuration — that of a big V-twin — is what produces the uneven power pulses that have become one of the classic Harley-Davidson trademarks. The concept, as we will see in the next section, has its roots much earlier in the century — and the lineage has resulted in a design that is markedly different to any other motor in production today.

These differences are evident throughout the Harley's construction. If we examine the bottom end for instance, we find that the crankshaft bearings are massively strong — two opposed taper rollers at one end, and two roller bearings at the other. This means that the engine is fundamentally capable of handling huge amounts of power, as evidenced by the large numbers of nitro-burning Harley drag bikes around the world.

Another throwback to bygone design philosophies is that the motor is built with no "design life" — in other words it's been designed to last as long as the owner wants it to. To this end, every bearing, shim, stud and dowel is replaceable. Most other makes have their components replaceable to a certain extent, but there often comes a time when it's no longer economically

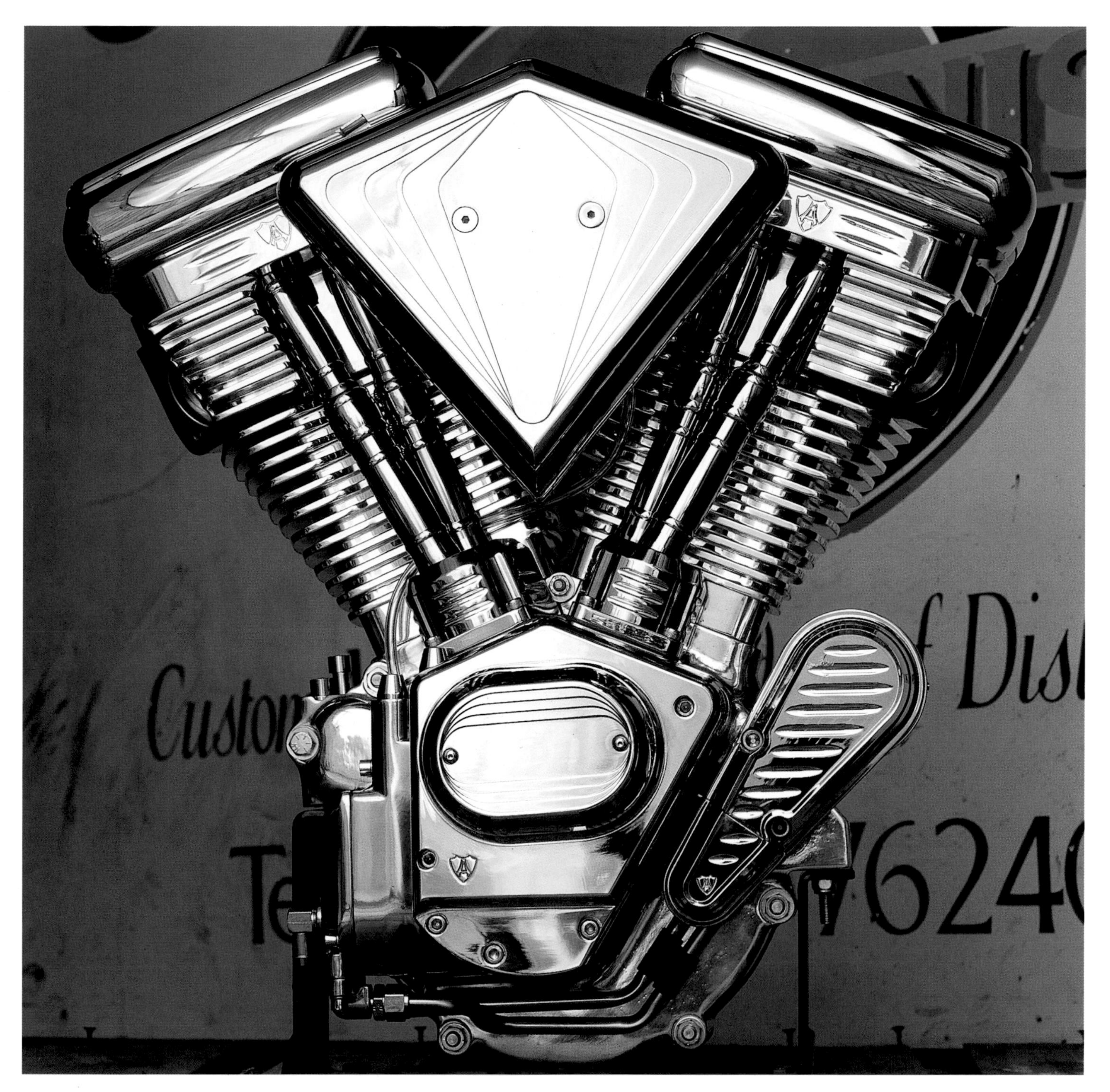

ABOVE: Gearcase and oil pump characterize the Harley bottom end. These and the lifter block/pushrod assemblies are easily accessible.

LEFT: Primary transmission is also easily accessible, something that makes Harleys very practical to work on for the home mechanic.

viable to do so. Another feature of the Harley motor, dating back to its earliest ancestors, is that the gearcase is easily accessible without a major engine teardown. As it carries the camshaft, the lifters, and the drive mechanism for the oil pump, we can access these parts whenever necessary.

Their "unlimited lifespan" is one of the reasons that secondhand Harley-Davidsons hold their values so well. It also means that spending money on customizing them won't be wasted by the bike running out of lifetime. All these and many more reasons make the Harley-Davidson very attractive for long term ownership, especially if it's to be customized.

I have been asked many, many times why I chose to build a Harley. I give various answers depending on who's asking. Sometimes I say it's because I'm an engineer, and I have a great respect for the way the Harley motor is built. Sometimes I say it's worth owning just for the noise it makes, and sometimes I say that I love the power curve that only a big V-twin can supply. At the end of the day though, there's a famous saying that sums it all up: "If you have to ask, you wouldn't understand!"

MARQUE HISTORY

Let's take a look at the background to all this, the motorcycle itself — the Harley-Davidson. The history of the marque is well documented. The company was born when the brothers Walter and William Davidson teamed up with William Harley to make a powered bicycle in 1903. The "factory" was a small wooden shed in Milwaukee. From these humble beginnings, the factory rose gradually over the years, with the first V-twin being produced in 1907. The engine was a "Flathead" design — meaning that it had side-valve construction.

The company's fortunes went up and down over the next three decades: it produced huge numbers of bikes for the war effort between 1914 and 1918; the Great Depression had an enormous effect on every facet of life in the late 1920s, and the Harley factory was no exception. Somehow it struggled through these bad times into the 1930s, when the direct ancestral lineage of the 1990s' Big Twin began.

In 1936 the Knucklehead was born, the first production overhead-valve V-twin, and the start of what has culminated today with the appropriately named Evolution. What would Darwin have made of it I wonder? The Knucklehead introduced many features with which we are familiar today — in fact the general layout hasn't changed at all.

The Panhead was introduced in 1948 as the successor to the "Knuck." This featured hydraulic lifters, which required no adjustment, and generated much less mechanical noise. It also had aluminum alloy heads, which meant the motor ran a lot cooler, with a resultant boost in reliability. The 1949 model had hydraulic forks, a major improvement for riding along the rough roads of the day; it was christened the Hydra-Glide. Then in 1952 the hand clutch came along, something most of us take for granted these days. The success of the Hydra-Glide was further improved in 1958, with the Duo-Glide. This had hydraulic suspension on the front and rear, with what is now considered a very conventional swing arm and twin shocks. The "Pan" gained an electric start in 1965 — its last year of production — on what has become one of Harley-Davidson's most famous models — the Electra-Glide.

ABOVE and LEFT: This post-war (1948) 74cu. in. bike (ABOVE) has clearly had an influence on the 1979 FLH Shovelhead (LEFT). Harley owners are very traditional and have resisted many changes in style proposed by the factory, which accounts for the marked similarity.

FAR LEFT: Early Harleys had to live with unmade roads, and instilled a pioneeer spirit. This 1908 single-cylinder Harley-Davidson would have been worked on to keep it running rather than for customizing. This proud owner is none other than Walter Davidson Sr. whose name is revered to this day.

Mention of the name Panhead among Harley lovers is guaranteed to raise nostalgic comments and a misty eye. For some reason it seems to be *the* bike many would choose to own if they had the cash to have another Harley. In 1966 the "Pan" was replaced by the Shovelhead, which had more horsepower because of yet more changes to the heads, but there were still those who mourned the loss of the old Panhead.

The decade of the 1960s was a time of great change for motorcycling, with a rising tide of reliable consumer products coming from Japan — the American and British motorcycle industries were swamped and both suffered heavily. In 1969 Harley-Davidson was in a weak position and unable to resist a take-over by AMF. For many enthusiasts this spelled the end of an era, with the new owners showing little interest or understanding of the unique demands of their customers. This also affected the workforce, who were consequently disillusioned. During the period of AMF's ownership, Harley-Davidson's reputation suffered, with a loss of reliability and quality control. There were a few bright spots, however — one of the great classics of all time made its first appearance in the model line-up in 1971, when the Super Glide was born. It was Harley-Davidson's first factory custom and it set the scene for years to come.

The sad years of AMF's ownership ended in 1981 with a management buyout. At this time another classic saw the light of day — the FXR. In 1983 the XR1000 was released, which was a Sportster designed to appeal to the performance market. It had twin carbs and high-level exhausts, and was clearly influenced by the XR750 dirt-tracker, and the famous road racer known as "Lucifer's Hammer."

1984 saw the biggest change for many years, with the Evolution engine, known as the "V2" by some, and as the "Blockhead" by others. It had aluminum alloy cylinders, new heads, and a host of detail changes. As with the change from the Pan to the Shovel, the new motor was not universally accepted: it soon got nicknamed the "Blockhead," on account of its squared-off looks — but once the new motor had been around a while, it found approval with all but the most die-hard of Shovelhead enthusiasts.

This new powertrain was the result of extensive development, with state-of-the-art technology being sought from various international companies, including pistons from Mahle in Germany, one of the world's leading suppliers, and a new clutch commissioned from A.P. Lockheed, in Coventry, England. Extra test and development facilities came from Ricardo

Consulting Engineers near Brighton, on the south coast of England. This company has been associated with the Harley-Davidson factory since 1915, when Harry Ricardo managed to get 55bhp from the 61cu.in. Model 17 eight-valve race-bike. Ricardo's reputation over the years has been maintained as specialists in the field of combustion processes. The company was subsequently contracted to assist with the Evolution engine, and tested late development prototypes in 1983.

As this book is written in 1997, the factory is publicly discussing the possibility of straying from the path of a "V-twins only" policy. This is mostly due to the ever-tightening emissions' laws, which make it almost impossible to manufacture a big air-cooled V-twin. Changing worldwide customer demands are also partly responsible, as European sportbikes are getting increasingly popular. Fortunately there's no question of stopping the production of V-twins in the near future. If the factory does decide to go ahead and develop a new range of bikes with some other configuration, there's one thing for sure — the V-twin Harley will remain the number one choice of customizers for years to come.

ABOVE: The 1950s are still evident in this 1990s Heritage Softail Classic FLSTC. The old styling is blended with the modern suspension of the Softail and its Evolution powertrain. Customizing alterations would be focused on freeing up the motor from pollution regulations (within the tolerances of state legislation).

HARLEY TYPES

There are basically two types of Harley-Davidson — the Sportster, and the Big Twin. The most easily recognized differences are that the Sportster has the engine and transmission in one unit, whereas the Big Twin has them separate. It also has the chain on the left, whereas the Sportster's is on the right.

Engine capacities for Harleys are quoted in cubic inches (cu. in.), whereas imports are referred to in cubic centimeters (cc). 74cu. in. equates to 1,200cc, and 80cu. in. to 1,340cc. Current capacities for the Sportster are 883cc and 1,200cc. Both bikes share the same crank, with a stroke of 3.812in, meaning that a hop-up from 883cc to 1,200cc is quite straightforward. The stock Big Twin has a capacity of 1,340cc.

Style separates Harleys from each other more than anything else, though. There are many different types — for instance in the Big Twin line-up alone there are such markedly different bikes as the Fatboy, the Heritage, and the Super Glide. On top of this, there are many more types of Harleys than just those offered in the factory line-up. There's an expression which states "form follows function," which is also particularly true when it comes to motorcycles: let us now take a look at some examples of the functions and the forms required for them.

Classic chops can have quite different styles, as shown by these two Shovels, even though they share many things like rigid frames, wide-glide triple trees and straight pipes.

ABOVE: A long front end with fat front wheel gives the stretched look.

BELOW: A short front end with skinny wheel makes a bike that's closer to a lowrider.

Drag racing

Harleys have always been popular in drag racing, which is similar in some ways to stop-light racing. Two bikes pull up on a start line, and when a light turns green they race along a straight track to the finish, a distance of usually a quarter mile. A fast street bike will make it in less than 12 seconds, whereas a top-fuel drag racer will take about seven. The street bike will be doing something like 110mph, but the top-fueler will be doing around 200mph! Customizers were not slow to recognize drag racing as a good source of high performance parts, so its big influence over the years is not surprising. There is another very similar form of racing called sprinting — it is much the same, but the bikes go one at a time.

Dirt-track racing

This is done on XR750s, usually on oval, cinder-covered circuits. Many people run Harleys down for being low performance bikes, but they clearly don't know that the XR750 is the single most successful racing bike in history, with more wins to its name than any other motorcycle. Many great names in road racing started out on Harley dirt-trackers — some, like Jay Springsteen, still ride them.

Road racing

This involves many riders competing around a twisting, paved circuit. Track lengths are quite variable — the longest in the world is the Isle of Man TT circuit, at 37 miles. The Harley-Davidson factory has built many road racers over the years, perhaps the most illustrious of which are the KR750, and the XRTT. Both were based on the XR750 dirt-track racer. Not so well known were the RR500 and RR250, which were the result of Harley's tie-up with Aermacchi — the 250 was produced in 1974, and the 500 in 1975. These were both two-strokes, so were a real departure from the V-twins normally associated with the Harley-Davidson name.

Dirt hillclimb

These bikes are built to race up a dirt hillside. The most famous of these is called the "Widowmaker." The bikes are often modified motocrossers, but a lot of Harleys are also used. They usually feature extended swing arms, and often run exotic fuels like nitro.

Speed hillclimb

These are not to be confused with dirt hillclimbers. They're built for a sort of uphill drag racing with corners. The paved tracks are variable in length, averaging

ABOVE: Trikes are very popular for many reasons — some riders want to carry loads or pull a trailer; others may have a disability preventing them from riding a solo.

BELOW: My bike — as radically different from custom Harleys as you can get. This bike is a speed hillclimb racer, built for short-distance sprint events. Featured in more detail later in the book, it has a heavily modified Evolution Big Twin motor installed in a one-off frame, with Grand Prix wheels and suspension.

BOTTOM: This bike is a Harley dirt-track racer. In the smaller classes single-cylinder engines like this one are used; in the larger classes these are replaced by V-twin XR750s.

The hot rod influence stems from the 1960s when the 900 Sporty ruled the roost across America. Many riders want to be able to ride their bikes hard, and so build with performance as a major factor.

RIGHT: The styling on this Sportster harks straight back to the 1960s, but it is built with up-to-the-minute parts such as modern forks and brakes.

BELOW: This Evolution Big Twin has 1990s' performance componentry tastefully blended with a custom style.

about a mile. This form of racing is common in Europe, but also happens elsewhere in the world. A few Harleys compete in sprint hillclimbs; I have used mine for 10 years.

Speed record bikes

These are run at places like the Bonneville salt flats. They compete in different classes and try to better their respective records. Over the years many Harleys have been used for land speed events, such as that driven by the late Cal Rayborn which set a record at 265mph, powered by an 89cu. in. Sportster motor. This bike was what's known as a streamliner — it looked like a cigar lying on its side.

Hot rods

Many road performance bikes are built around Sportsters, often in the style of dirt-trackers or café racers, whereas Big Twins usually mimic drag racers. Handling and engine performance are the main priorities and the bikes are often referred to as "Hot Rods."

Touring bikes

As the name implies, these are built to go long distances. They're usually fitted with windshields and luggage-carrying capacity. The priority here is a motor with a big, fat, lazy feel, so the emphasis is on torque rather than horsepower.

Retros

Those machines, styled after the look of old bikes are known as "Retros." The factory has built its own version with the Heritage Softail.

Custom bikes

When people hear the word custom, a "Chop" is what usually springs to mind. There are many different styles, from the classic 1970s' look (rigid frame, high bars, long exhausts, small gas tank) through to Swedish chops — radically styled bikes, with high headstocks and very long front ends. The "Fatboy" look is another example of modern custom bike styling. These are built to look wide, including the seat, gas tanks, fenders, lights, etc. The lowrider style has been popular for years: one particular version was the "Bay Area Lowrider," named after a series of bikes built around San Francisco.

Vintage bikes

The word "vintage" can refer to the actual age of a bike, or to its styling. The look of bikes from the 1920s and 1930s was quite distinctive, and some builders have chosen to emulate this with old-age looks and a modern powerplant.

BELOW: This Big Dog is built as a retro with fishtail exhausts, deep fenders, and many other parts to give it a period feel.

BEFORE YOU START

WORKSHOP REQUIREMENTS

If you're going to build a custom bike yourself, the very first thing you need to sort out is where you're going to build it. If you have a workshop, then there's no problem, but if you don't you're going to find things hard. I've built bikes in attics, living rooms, basements, garages, and factories, — the prime requisites are security, space, light, power, ventilation and a lack of damp or dust.

Once you've got that sorted out, you're going to need some tools: so let's examine what you should have, and what you can get away without. The list of usual hand tools goes without saying — I'm talking about wrenches, screwdrivers, sockets, etc — but what about the more serious things, such as power tools? Well, for my own custom building I have the following: lathe, milling machine, MIG welder, oxy-acetylene welding set, plasma cutter, bench grinder, bandsaw, bench spindle polisher, frame jig, and a compressor.

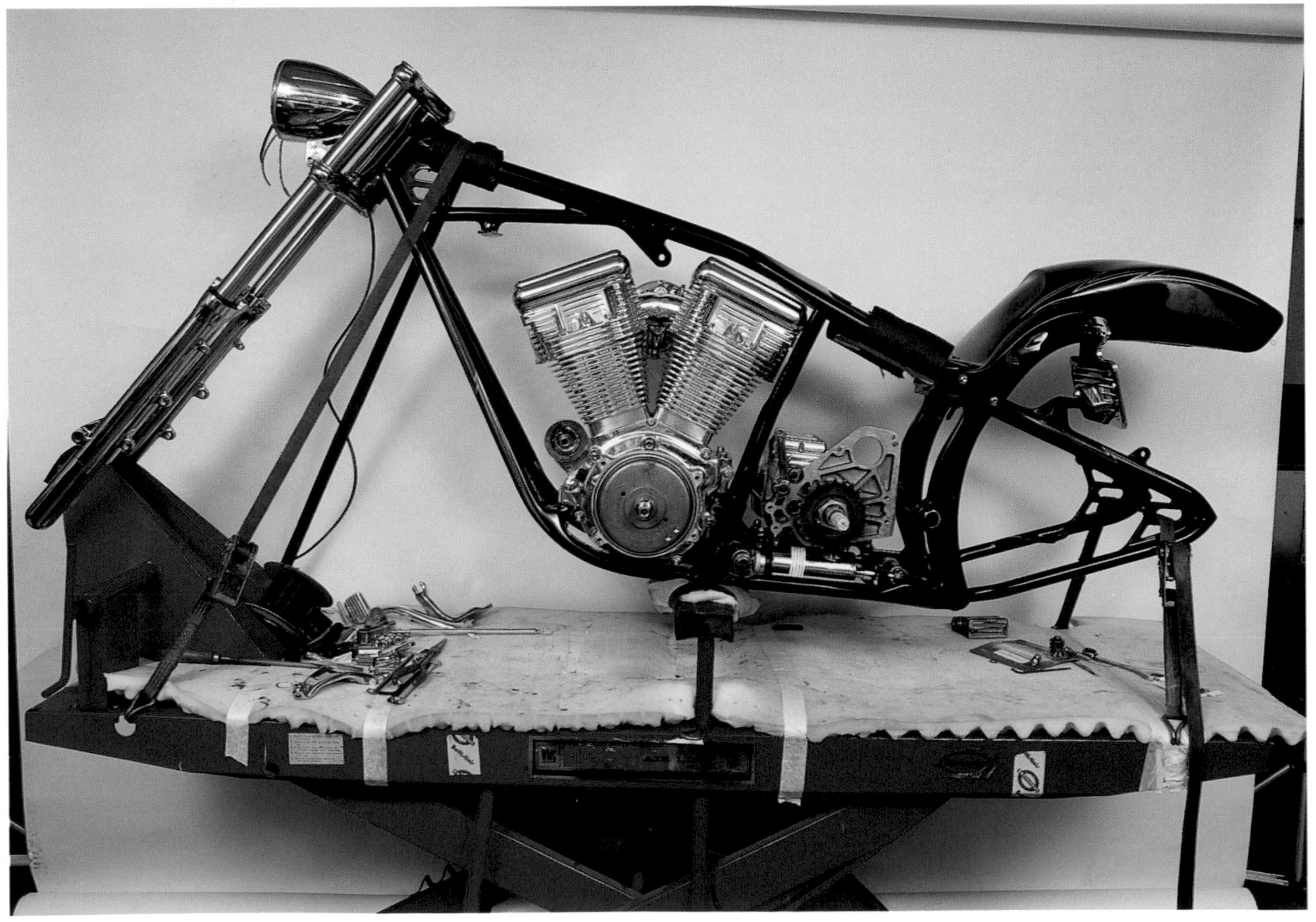

ABOVE: In the Battistinis' workshop, this bike has a spotlight clamped in place at the back to give the builder enough light to work professionally. A well laid-out, clean workshop is a most important assset, although it needn't be a dull place, as can be seen here.

ABOVE LEFT: Nothing beats a Big Twin motor as a powerplant or as a piece of art! If you're working on a motor, get a stand to keep it secure, or it'll fall over and do some damage.

BELOW LEFT: This bike is being worked on professionally in the Battistinis' workshop. There's a proper workbench with plenty of space to get at everything. It has good lighting and is in a clean workshop. Note that the frame is well secured, and has cloth protection for the paintwork.

The latter powers a variety of air tools like die grinders, hand linishers, socket guns, spray guns, tire inflating equipment, etc. — but most important of all is a small nozzle for clearing blocked jets and oilways. I also have a wide variety of electric hand tools — drills, soldering irons, grinders, etc.

There is a category of products in the workshop called consumables, which includes anything that gets used up, but which doesn't come under components or raw materials. It can include anything from hand cleaner to solder. If you're going to have a peaceful and trouble-free time while you construct your bike, you're going to need a good supply of consumables. While you're at the planning stage you should be listing what you have, and what you don't, so that you can get them before you start. Don't forget that products can "go bad" over the years, especially if they have been stored in direct sunlight. There are few things as frustrating as having to stop half-way through a job because you forgot to stock up on some vital compound: it usually takes hours to figure out some way of doing without something you could easily have bought earlier. The list of consumables could include things like thread-locking compounds, silicone gasket sealant, cleaning solvents, assembly lubricants, metal polish, valve grinding paste, and a whole host of products to do with painting — things like masking tape, rubbing compound, primer, thinners, and so on.

We'll visit the subject of nuts and bolts in detail in a later section, but while you're checking out your current stock of consumables, have a look to see how you're off for fasteners. A good supply of nuts and bolts will last you for years if kept dry — some of the ones in my collection have been there for over 20 years, but I'll sure need them some day!

Something that you must bear in mind is the fact that the workshop can be a very dangerous place for the lazy or the inept. You can't build your bike if you're in hospital. One of the easiest ways to seriously injure yourself is to use tools like grinders without eye protection. Believe me, I know — when I was young and stupid I managed to get a metal splinter in my eye through being too lazy to reach for the goggles. I only had a quick bit of grinding to do, and they were all the way over the other side of the workshop. Boy, did I wish I'd taken the trouble when I was in a hospital chair with a surgeon digging about in my eye with a long needle!

There are lots of ways to hurt yourself using tools. The surest recipe for disaster is to be in a hurry. Even something as simple as picking up a dropped part can be dangerous — are you standing near any rotating machinery? Unsecured hair can drag you into serious trouble. If you're bending over, and you stand up without checking, you can easily hit your head. A milling machine is big and heavy — it won't give, but your skull will. Take care, take your time, and be the envy of your friends with your creations.

If you're going to perform major work on your chassis, you may well need access to a frame jig to keep things straight and true. These can be as complicated, or as simple, as you want to make them. I've seen examples made from everything from steel girders to old lathe beds. There are two vital things to watch out for — whatever you construct must be accurate and stable. By "stable" I mean that when you start welding, it must be strong enough to keep the frame straight without distortion. Be aware that welding can create enormous stresses in steel tubes. Accuracy is needed in a frame jig to ensure the various components are aligned correctly. Things like the angles of the forks and swing arm are less important than keeping the main shafts parallel and horizontal. These include the crank, the transmission mainshaft, and the swing arm and wheel axles. The most critical thing is they must all be truly "square" — that is at 90° to the steering head.

Another jig which can make your life easier is an engine stand. It's amazing how many people chase their motor all over the workbench as they work on it. A good stand will hold it firm, allowing you to work with a lot more precision. They're easy to construct — you can use anything from wood to steel. Next time you're near Harley mechanics, take a good look at what they use.

If you're going to perform a lot of custom work yourself, you'll need some welding equipment. There are three different types of welding that are suitable for frame work — MIG, TIG and Oxy-Acetylene. MIG — metal inert gas — is where a gun held by the operator feeds a wire continuously to the weld site. The part being welded is connected to an earth clamp, and the welding wire is connected to an electrical supply which melts it on contact. The "inert gas" referred to is either carbon dioxide or argon. This forms a "gas

shield" around the weld, to prevent oxygen contamination. Argon gives a better quality result.

TIG — tungsten inert gas — is very similar to MIG. Here the operator holds a gun with a fixed tungsten electrode in one hand, and a filler wire in the other. The more expensive systems have a foot control, but sometimes a thumb switch is used instead. With this level of welding, argon is always used as the inert gas. The differences between MIG and TIG are that MIG is good for general construction work — garden gates, car bodies, stock Harley frames, etc. TIG is much more clinical, and is used to build aircraft, racing cars/bikes, etc.

Gas welding is going out of fashion these days, but in the right hands some very good work can be produced. Even if you have some other form of welder, it's worth having a set of gas bottles and torches — there will be many occasions when you'll need to heat a seized component to free it. A cutting torch, often called a "gas axe," can also save the day when heavy construction work is undertaken.

You don't need this much equipment, but it really does help. It has taken me many years to collect my tools, and I guess I'll go on collecting until the day I meet the great customizer in the sky! When I started out I had only the most basic equipment — I didn't even have an electric hand drill: it's amazing what can be done with just a few files, a hacksaw, some other simple tools, and dedication. If you're prepared to do things the hard way, you'll learn a great deal, and you'll really get to admire what was done by the pioneers of engineering before power tools were invented. These guys made some really intricate things — think about how clocks were made for instance. It's also a lot harder to do the wrong thing when it takes you hours, instead of seconds, to do an operation. I think all customizers should learn their engineering this way.

If you're fortunate enough to own, or have access to, a machine shop, then the sky's the limit to what you can make for your bike. There are only three things that can hold you back — your experience, your confidence, and your imagination. Something that's always fascinated me is that all the really good machinists I've met are also good artists. They may not sit out in fields with oil paints and a canvas, but they all have an inherent feel for "form," how a line should flow, and a feel for proportion. There is obviously a case for saying there's no real line between art and engineering.

LEFT: A small lathe like this Myford can be used in the home workshop as well as in a commercial establishment.

BELOW: It takes years to build up a set of tools like this!

WHAT TO SUBCONTRACT

At some stage you're going to have to pay someone else to perform tasks for you. This may be because you don't have the right experience, or because you don't have the right equipment. Let's examine what these operations might be.

It's very unlikely that the home customizer is going to have his own chrome plating equipment, so I'll assume that this will be farmed out. If you don't own a machine polisher, or know someone who has one, then this is another expense you're gong to have to deal with. Depending on what type of custom you're building, you're going to have to decide how good your paint job needs to be. If you want to compete in shows, you're going to have to ensure that you have some quality work done, something that will require the attentions of a professional spray artist.

The area where most people will get stuck is in building the engine. To do a really good job, some expensive and specialized equipment is required. Very few home mechanics have the sort of tools to check cylinder wear to 1/10,000 of an inch. These sorts of tolerances may seem over the top, but if you want the best Harley motor around (and who doesn't?) it's definitely worth the extra time and trouble.

Another piece of specialized gear is the power hone, which is used to size things like the big end and the pinion shaft-bearing sleeve — again this search for accuracy is what sets the men apart from the boys. Likewise, good reboring and cylinder honing facilities are usually beyond the scope of the home garage.

The equipment required to balance and true a crankshaft is not expensive, but it is a job best left to a professional: getting this job wrong is disastrous. Porting and gasflowing are expressions used to describe more or less the same thing — specialized cylinder-head work. This may include the replacement of valve seats — if a seat works loose serious engine damage will result, so it needs to be done correctly, a job which requires some tooling that is way beyond home wrenching.

At one time there were many motorcycle shops that built wheels. These days though, wheel-building is a dying skill. It doesn't require specialized tools, but it does require a certain amount of experience and patience. If you fancy trying it, find some old spoked

LEFT and RIGHT: Whatever your tastes may be, unless you're a really good artist you're going to have to subcontract work like this. The equipment needed to spray modern toxic paints is specialist and expensive.

BELOW: Don't rush jobs like molding, as you'll need to strip the whole bike to re-do it. Here Rick James of Battistinis takes his time to get it right, applying just enough filler to do the job. If too much is used, it's likely to crack and fall out through vibration.

wheels in a wrecking yard, and practice dismantling and rebuilding them. If you get good at it, you can even subsidize your customizing costs by earning some extra cash with your new found skill!

Sooner or later you're going to need to get some general machining work done. This may be milling work, such as boring out triple trees, or it may be lathe work, such as wheel spacers. If you don't have either of these machine tools, then you're going to have to find someone to do the work for you.

It helps a lot to understand what's involved in a machining operation before you ask someone to perform it for you. If you don't know enough about it, you're likely to end up getting the wrong thing made. While some machinists are excellent engineers, many have little comprehension beyond operating their particular piece of equipment. This means that you risk getting what you asked for, even if it's the wrong thing — so get advice first.

The conclusion to this section is that whenever you need to get outside work done, follow these golden rules:

• If you don't fully understand what you need done, find out first from someone who does. Make sure that the person giving you the advice is impartial — in other words, that they don't stand to make any money from you.

• Once you know enough to go ahead and get the job done, find out who in your area can perform the work. Then ask around to get recommendations — good or bad. Find out about standards of workmanship. Find out about delivery times: many places will quote short times just to get the work, but once they've got it, deadlines can get moved back and back.

• Lastly, remember you get what you pay for, so don't go basing your choice entirely on cost. You can't beat the recommendation of satisfied customers. There's a saying that if you want the job done well, give it to the busiest man in town!

BELOW: Arlen Ness is one of the world leaders in customizing Harleys for over 30 years. The company name is synonymous with quality workmanship. This bike is at the very pinnacle of motorcycle art: if you want to emulate this success, you will have to learn to plan every detail meticulously. This will include to whom you are going to subcontract the painting, plating, polishing, engine building, and any other specialist services.

PLANNING

The amount of planning you'll need to do depends on the level of customization you intend to perform. It also depends on four major factors — time, money, skill, and facilities. If you have the money you can do without the other three — you just go to a custom shop, and ask them to build your bike for you, right? Wrong! If you turn up at any old shop you *could* strike lucky, but then you probably won't. Even if you do strike lucky, it's highly unlikely that the bike that gets built will be what you want unless you've talked it through with the builder first — so you still need to do some planning.

We'll take an overview of what needs planning now, but the more detailed aspects will be examined at each stage throughout the book. It's not possible to set out an exact timetable as things will go wrong — parts won't fit, suppliers won't deliver on time, and you'll take longer to do things than you thought possible. There's a rule of thumb when it comes to customizing: if you multiply the cost and time estimates by three, the chances are that you'll probably be somewhere near the real figures.

If you don't know exactly what you want, you need to do some research. If you're wondering where to start, there are two good sources to begin with — people and books. If you know people who are into Harleys you won't need much prompting, because as with every other Harley rider in the world, Harley-Davidson bikes will be the main topic of conversation anyway. If you don't know many bikers in your area, it's time to start reading. Take out a subscription to *Hot Bike*, and read every issue cover to cover. Find and purchase every Harley book that looks like it might have something to say, and read it.

BELOW: We don't know who built this, or why — we don't even know what it is and we don't want to be rude about it, but if you want to get your bike looking the way you want it, you're going to have to plan ahead.

ABOVE RIGHT: This bike, "Corsa" by Battistinis, is an excellent example of detailed forward planning.

BELOW RIGHT: This is the most fundamental stage of any custom bike — the dry build. Here's where you check fits and clearances. Note careful use of tape and plastic to protect delicate surfaces, and markings where changes are needed.

ABOVE: Unfortunately you can't just "chrome" an engine — every part needs careful thought. Ask yourself (or someone qualified) questions like "Does this thread need masking off?" "How about that gasket face?" "Will this part still fit when the plating is done?" . . . and so on. A successfully built motor will need to look good AND run well, so think ahead.

RIGHT: More examples of workmanship that required a lot of forethought — intricate paintwork, engraving, and gold-plating are not jobs for amateurs.

PREVIOUS PAGE: If you want to create something with a motor like this, you're going to have to make sure that all the parts match properly, or else you're going to have an expensive blow-up! This bike belongs to Big Al of Big Dog Motorcycles, Witchita, Kansas.

The planning stage needs to be done over a period of time so that no hasty decisions are made. The list of considerations must include things such as whether the bike you're going to customize is your only form of transport — do you need your bike for work? Building a custom takes a lot of time and money. If you can't work, you can't earn; so unless you have a nest egg stashed away, you're going to have to plan your customizing around weekends and holidays. This automatically means that you're going to have to perform lots of small modifications, rather than one big one.

The "one piece at a time" route is often the best way to go for someone inexperienced at customizing — it means that keeping track of such things as financial outlay is much easier. Each step of the way you've plenty of time to think about what to do next, and to seek advice if necessary. It's also an excellent way of feeling for yourself the effect of each and every modification. It's a good way of learning, and an even better way of setting the bike up to make the best of each change — and a side effect is how rewarding it is to feel your bike evolve under you over the months or even years of modifications.

For those of you who have some drafting skills, it may be a good idea to draw up some plans of the bike you're going to build. Those who don't draw too well still ought to make some sketches of their intended project. Something all too many inexperienced customizers overlook is how important it is to plan an overall shape to the bike. A drawn plan — never mind how crude — will help this process.

As far as when to start is concerned, for those who live in the north there is an enforced break in the riding season every fall, so this is the best time to tear the bike down and work on it. The onset of spring is a time of panic the world over, as riders desperately try to get their bikes ready for that first sunny day!

One of the golden rules when it comes to planning a custom project is "Don't believe the hype." There are so many claims made for every component in the marketplace: don't get taken in by them. Keep a cool head, and take your time before parting with your cash. If you can, find someone who has already used the parts you're planning to use, and seek their opinion — but be careful: you'll have to judge carefully how reliable their comments are, as not many people like to admit they bought the wrong thing.

In the markets of ancient Rome it was customary to have a sign at the entrance saying *Caveat Emptor.* This translates as "Let the buyer beware" — two thousand years later it's still good advice.

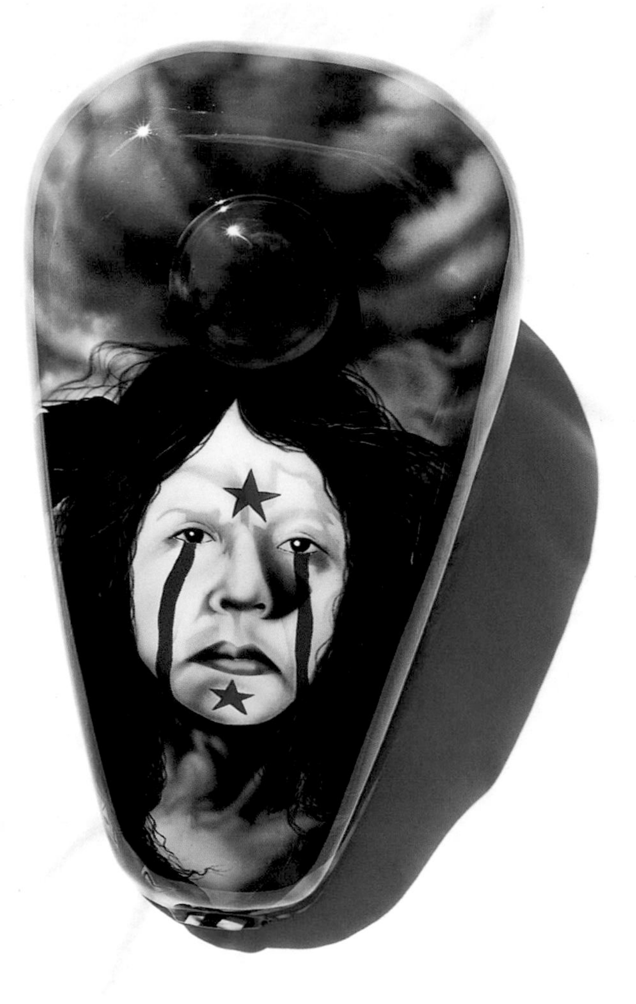

CUSTOMIZING YOUR HARLEY

ENGINES

TOP: This Battistinis' bike has a beautifully built Evo Big Twin motor with Edelbrock heads and a multitude of billet engine covers.

ABOVE: And here's another Evo Big Twin, this time seen from the chaincase side.

Almost every Harley motor gets modified in some way during its life. We'll take a look now at what choices there are, and what decisions need to be made before you start spending money. The Evolution is the bike most likely to be worked on, but the following applies to the rest of the range as well.

The bottom end has changed very little over the years, with most of the changes being to the cylinders and heads. For a start, the current oiling system was never designed from scratch — it has evolved from the pre-World War II era — but despite its age, it does work very well.

There are many possible routes in the search for engine improvements. Most people read improvements to mean "more performance" — believe it or not there are riders who aren't interested in going faster. Mostly, they want more reliability, and increased ability to haul a side-hack, or heavyweight tourer.

Whatever the goal, the first decision is how big to make the motor. The usual axiom is that there's "no substitute for cubes" — in that more cubic capacity equals more horsepower. To a certain extent this is true — until you start to get really technical, which I'll come back to.

There are three major categories to look at when choosing your engine capacity:

- Leave it standard: in the case of Evolution Big Twins, this is 80cu. in. (1,340cc). This will suit many owners. Firstly it's the easy option, and secondly it's also the cheapest.

- Make it bigger. This can be done by stroking (increasing the throw of the crankshaft) and by boring (bigger pistons) — or you can combine the two. When the stroke is increased, there is a commensurate increase in piston speed — the pistons have to go further, so they go faster. This has its problems, as we'll see.

- Make it smaller. This might sound a bit strange, but has its advantages. If you lower the stroke, the pistons don't have to go so far. As piston speed is the limiting factor to horsepower in most engines, this means you can rev the motor harder without reaching the maximum piston speed. If you want a real hot rod, the answer is to fit a short-stroke crank and bigger pistons. This way you get back most of the capacity you lost by dropping the stroke.

ABOVE LEFT: The cylinder head has a huge influence on the power produced by a motor. Edelbrock have been in the automotive business for many, many years manufacturing quality components.

ABOVE: The Sportster motor has many fans in the high performance field.

Why go to this trouble? Well, as mentioned earlier, it gets technical — cylinder heads are what govern the amount of fuel/air mix that gets into the motor. More mix means more horsepower, no matter what the actual capacity is. The flow rate of a motor is linked to the natural frequency of its intake ports, which is also related to the rpm.

A modified two-valve head as fitted to an Evo Big Twin doesn't reach its optimum flow rate until somewhere in the region of 7,300rpm. Unfortunately, the piston speed of a stock-stroke motor is already well past the limit at 6,000rpm. So, to get those heads flowing properly, you need lots of revs. This won't concern the average road rider, but for someone building a killer custom, it may be very important.

So, these are the basic choices — leave it the same, make it bigger, or make it smaller. The level of skill required to build custom engine capacities can be immense, so unless you are really experienced *and* have access to a serious engine building facility, leave it to the professionals. There are many shops around which can supply ready-to-run engines, to the capacity of your choice.

There are certain routes to bigger engines that are within the technical reach of those who want to turn the wrenches themselves. The best of these is to fit a big-bore kit. These come complete with all the necessary hardware required for installation and it should include comprehensive fitting instructions and sometimes even a video as well. One of the advantages of modern engineering techniques is that in recent years some really nice equipment has come on the market — cylinders, pistons, cams, cases, etc. In fact one of the biggest problems is wading through all the choices we have open to us!

The next issue to look at is stress. With any increase in bhp, there is also an increase in stress on the rest of the motor. The most critical components are the crank cases. Stock cases have been known to split, usually along the right-hand side next to the lifter blocks. There are many companies who offer replacements — such as S&S and Delkron. The aftermarket versions were first developed for drag-racing, where the stresses of running nitromethane fuels will blow anything apart that's not up to the job. This means for high performance road use they'll last for ever and a day.

ABOVE: Another Sportster motor, this time with cylinders by Axtell, long renowned for bullet-proof engine parts. The billet canister at the front of the motor is an oil filter housing. The large billet unit on the side of the cylinders houses the ignition coils.

RIGHT: High performance parts are available for all Harley Big Twins, but for some of the older models it may be a better idea to go for durability, rather than power. For instance, improvements made to oil filtration and cooling would pay dividends, especially if you live somewhere like the Nevada desert.

There are many choices of cases out there, but they can all be divided into two categories: cast and billet. The latter would survive anything short of a nuclear strike, but are outside the financial reach (and requirements) of most road riders. I have been running cast cases on my race motor for 10 years without a failure.

As mentioned previously, piston speed increases with revs. If you double the revs, the load on the connecting rods is squared. This means that a small increase in revs gives a massive increase in load on the rods. While they may be safe for continued use at say, 5,500rpm, they could be unsafe at 6,500rpm for any length of time. Start turning the motor over 7,000rpm and you're asking for trouble. There are some excellent replacements on the market, examples of which include Carillo and S&S.

We are now getting into a situation where we are looking at buying cases, crank, rods, pistons and cylinders. If you're doing all this, you're going to need some serious cylinder head work (porting or gasflowing). By the time you have shipped your heads off, paid a large sum of money, and then waited months for them to come back, it makes a lot of sense to buy some high performance aftermarket items instead. This has the additional advantage that you can specify exactly what equipment you intend to run, and have the heads supplied more or less ready to fit.

If you decide to go this route, you have basically just replaced your entire motor. This means that you have a choice right from the outset. If you're building a bike from scratch it obviously makes sense to construct a motor from parts, rather than buy a motor and then strip it and replace everything. This also applies if you already have a bike which you are planning to customize. You need to decide at the start whether to sell the engine you have and use the money to buy the parts you need. You could even sell the entire bike and start from a clean sheet of paper.

What other engine parts are going to need replacing in the search for more horsepower? Well, for a start the pushrods are going to have to go. You're going to need some that will provide extra stiffness, and also they'll need to be adjustable. The stock items are fixed length, which is no help if you change the height of the cylinders, or if you get the heads machined down to gain compression ratio.

We haven't yet looked at what goes on in the cylinder heads. There are two basic types available in the aftermarket — two and four-valve. The heads supplied on a stock bike have two valves. This works very well, but for some race-engine builders there is no substitute for four valve heads. The theory is quite straightforward: you can fit more small valves into a combustion chamber than you can big ones. This means you get a lot of what's called "valve area." It's the main thing that governs how much fuel/air mix it's possible to get into the motor. Remember, it's the amount of mix drawn in that determines how much power you can get. Another advantage of small valves is that they're lighter. A light valve doesn't need as much valve spring pressure to control it as a heavy one. The lighter the valve spring, the less friction there is inside the motor, meaning less power is wasted.

There are many valve and spring combinations available. For the ultimate in racing use, there is nothing to beat titanium valves for lack of weight, but these have a very short lifespan — leave them in the motor too long and they'll fail. Unfortunately, their life

is too short for regular road use, and they are also prohibitively expensive. The same can be said for titanium con-rods. What's more, a failure of either will destroy your motor.

When choosing a valve and spring type, you need to have already chosen what cam you're going to run. It will determine the amount of lift the valves will experience, and this may limit the ones which are suitable for your application.

When building high performance heads you may want to fit some better quality rocker arms. These can be bought with "roller tips," which are designed to lower friction and side thrust on the valve stems. They're also made of higher quality materials and engineered to better tolerances — they're nice, but expensive.

ABOVE RIGHT: Ness-Tech "Radius Smooth" oil filter mount will clean up the look of a custom bike, and still be functional.

RIGHT: The stock filter screws into the housing before the cover is installed.

BELOW: Here a "grooved" oil filter mount can be seen on this part-built show bike. Note how the grooved theme is continued throughout the motor and transmission.

ABOVE: This 1987 1200cc Sportster has V8 cams, Andrews' gears and a Barnett clutch. Some pretty serious attention has been paid to lubrication with the fitting of an oil cooler to the front downtubes.

All these little bits add up. If you talk to a successful race-engine builder, you'll find they've achieved success by paying a lot of attention to detail. There is no magic in building high performance motorcycles — it just takes lots and lots of hard work, thought, and planning.

LUBRICATION

The next area to look at is lubrication. No engine, race or road, will last long without a good oiling system. Take as an example that of the Big Twin, the design of which goes back to 1936. It has evolved over the years and consequently the result is an effective, but rather strange system, which needs some careful thought if the ultimate in performance is desired. However, for road and mild strip use, the stock Evolution set-up will provide reliable use for many years, but it's worth fitting an aftermarket breather gear to help the crankcases vent properly.

For serious race use, the biggest drawback with the stock oil pump is that it doesn't scavenge the cases properly. In other words, it doesn't suck hard enough, leaving too much oil in the motor — so if a replacement is going to be fitted, this is its most important feature. You may be wondering why it's so important to get the oil out — surely we want the oil in the motor, not the oil tank? Well, one of the features of a Harley is its massive crank, which gives that power curve we all love. However, the payback is that it only takes a little drag on the edge of the flywheel to make a big difference to the horsepower. Too much oil in the crank cases creates a serious amount of drag. Under normal road riding conditions, it's of little concern as the motor isn't turning that fast anyway, but start spinning it at over 7,000rpm, and the oil pump just can't keep up.

If you choose to fit a replacement oil pump, be very careful. A faulty oil pump will ruin your motor — from my own experience I know that there are so-called performance pumps out there that have been badly made, and will lead to complete engine failure. If you don't need a bigger pump, leave the stock one in place. Alternatively, if you're really serious about horsepower, fit an extra pump to help scavenge the cases, a set with a sump plate pick-up (such as those by

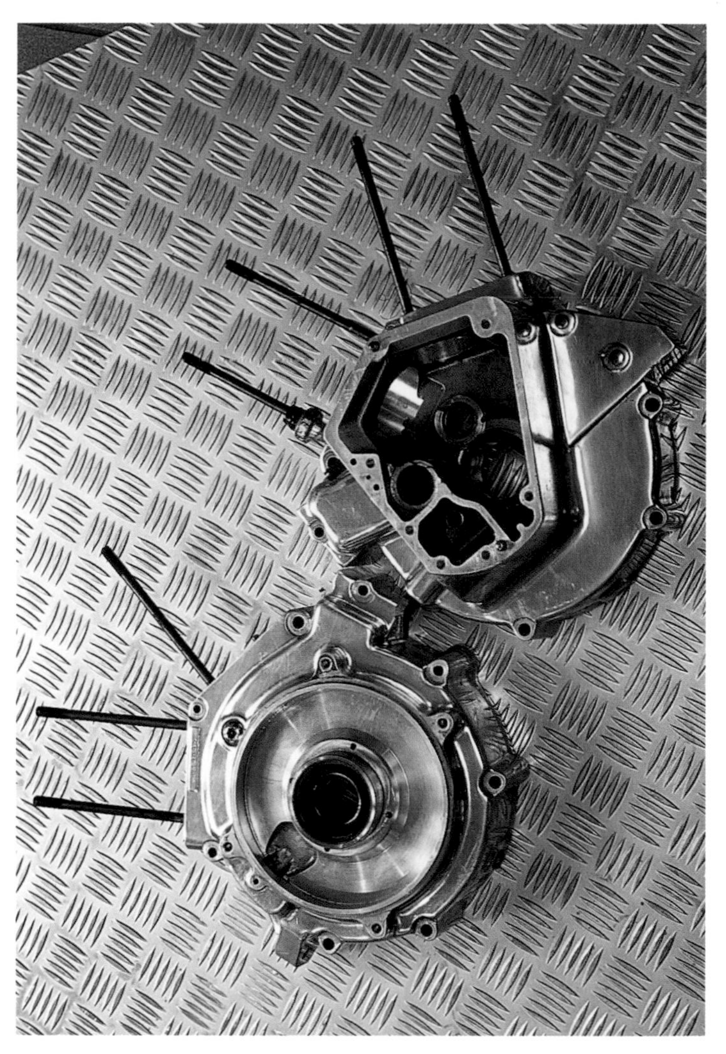

Delkron) is a real help here. For a drag bike you can use an electric fuel pump from a race car.

ABOVE LEFT: The crank in a Harley Big Twin has massive flywheels — it only needs a little oil drag on them to slow the motor considerably; if you're going drag racing make sure your scavenge system works well!

ABOVE: When installing a new cam, check that there's clearance between the lobes and the crankcase. If there's insufficient gap, use a die grinder to cut away some case material to suit your application. Check also that your breather window is fully open at the right time — if not, get that die grinder out again.

CAMSHAFTS

Let's take a look at some other gearcase components. On pre-Evolution engines tuned for performance, the hydraulic lifters were a source of trouble; this meant that they needed replacing with some decent alternatives. The Evo lifters, however, are far superior and will be fine for the road as well as for mild strip use.

I've mentioned cams, but it's worth looking at them in detail. The profile on a camshaft is what determines when the valves open, how far they open (lift), how long they stay open (duration), and when they close. These figures are quoted by the manufacturers in their sales material. Unfortunately, it's not as simple as just choosing a cam by numbers.

The easiest trap to fall into is to choose the "biggest" cam you can find. The fact of the matter is that you need to match the cam to your motor very carefully. It sometimes involves trying different cams to get just what you need. If you're running a motor with, say, a five-inch stroke, you're not going to be able to rev it very hard. This means that you can specify a cam with a lot of lift, which means a lot of fuel/air mix can get in. If you were to fit this type of cam to a high revving motor, however, you would tear the valve gear apart.

It's just not physically possible to accelerate a valve that's somewhere near two inches wide (and therefore heavy) at the rates necessary for this. If you want a high revver, you need less lift — but what you lose in lift you can gain with more duration.

Cams are made by many different manufacturers, for instance by Crane, Sifton, Andrews, RevTech, and, of course, they are also available through Harley's "Screaming Eagle" range. To illustrate the point, imagine we want to select a good cam for an Evolution-engined road bike. Straight away we know that we want something that'll fit straight in without major engine work. We also know that we want to run our

ABOVE LEFT: Carl's Speed Shop heads are slightly different to those above, as you can see in the shape of the combustion chamber. What you can't see is the shape of the ports. Every tuner has his own ideas and methods, so there's no simple answer to what is good, and what isn't.

ABOVE: The volume of the combustion chamber needs to be kept as small as possible to keep the compression ratio up. However, there is a trade-off: if the valves are masked by chamber material, you'll lose flow rate, which will also rob you of power. Here you can see the chamber is cut away near the sparkplug to increase flow in this area.

stock hydraulic lifters, as they need no maintenance, and run very quietly. This means we can narrow down our choice to something with less than five hundred thou of lift, and we can rule out solid lifter cams.

So an immediate shortlist becomes apparent, a representative example of which is shown below. The chart shows when the valves open and close, and their duration (how long they stay open). The value given for valve lift is just that, whereas some cams have their lobe height quoted instead. All the figures below were taken at 0.053in lift — which is the normal way of measuring cams.

	Open	Close	Duration	Valve lift
Andrews EV3				
Intake	21°	37°	238°	0.495in
Exhaust	43°	15°	238°	0.495in
Crane 326-2				
Intake	24°	48°	252°	0.490in
Exhaust	57°	25°	262°	0.500in
Sifton 140 EV				
Intake	30°	42°	252°	0.450in
Exhaust	55°	27°	262°	0.450in

Depending on who you talk to, you'll hear various comments for and against each of these types, but suffice it to say that they all perform much the same job, even with such different numbers. The best thing is to find someone who really knows what they're talking about, and take advice. The best person to find is a local drag racer. The odds are he started like you, and if you show him some respect, and choose the right time (not just before he sets up on the start line!), you might get to hear what you need to know.

When installing a cam there are various things to watch out for. If you have gone for lots of lift, check the lobes don't foul the crankcases. Check the valve gear will allow this amount of lift, check the valves are not going to hit the pistons, and that there is the right

ABOVE: These two-valve pistons are high performance items with low crowns, thin compression rings, and three-piece oil scrapers. This type is known as "slipper" pistons because of the machined-away areas around the wrist pins. This gives them low friction and low weight for maximum rpm.

end float clearance. And make extra sure you get the cam timing right, or you'll stick the valves straight through the pistons! Follow the manufacturer's installation recommendations, and you shouldn't go too wrong.

PISTONS

There's a vast array of choices available here, too. Every different engine builder has his own favorite brand: my personal choice is to go for those by Cosworth Engineering. They produce beautifully made, light, and accurate pistons for many of the really serious racing teams, such as those in Formula One and Indy Cars.

What is so important about piston design? A piston performs several functions, the most important of which is to help to provide a good seal against the pressure of combustion. It does this by giving the piston rings a nice stable location — if the rings can wobble around, they lose their contact with the cylinder wall, and therefore their ability to stop pressure leakage. To provide this stable location, the piston must be a good fit in the cylinder bore. Not too difficult to achieve, you might think, but the complication comes when the cylinders reach working temperature — everything expands at different rates and some things don't fit the same when they are hot as when they are cold. To get around this, the pistons must be made with the right amount of clearance or else they'll seize or rattle once warmed up — hence the importance of good design.

COMPRESSION RATIO

The pistons together with the combustion chamber volume also determine an engine's compression ratio. What is meant by compression ratio? It is the ratio between by how much the mixture is compressed when the pistons are at the top of their stroke, and when they are at the bottom of their stroke. On pre-Evolution engines the combustion chamber was very deep, which meant that to get enough "squeeze" of the fuel/air mix, the pistons had to have very domed crowns.

This gave the right compression ratio, but it had two major problems — the pistons became very heavy, and a domed crown absorbs a lot more heat than a flat one. If the piston absorbs heat, it expands more: if it expands too much, it will seize, so it has to be given more cylinder clearance. This means that it doesn't contact the cylinder properly anymore, so it loses some of its ring seal. More importantly though, it can't dissipate heat to the cylinder wall, so it heats up even more, needing more cylinder clearance . . .

Evolution engines, however, were designed with a far superior combustion chamber shape. It's not perfect, but it's still a much better design than before. The best way to increase the compression ratio is to lower the combustion chamber volume. This means either welding up the heads, and re-machining them to a new shape, or buying some that have been made to the right design. If you buy new ones, it gives you the advantage that was mentioned before, in that you won't have to wait ages for the work to be done by a specialist.

WEIGHT

One of the areas that often gets overlooked when seeking extra engine performance is the weight of its components. Anything that moves when the engine is running uses up precious horsepower: it might not be much, but all the same it's wasting power either through friction, or through inertia. If you're building a long distance tourer, you won't care about getting the maximum possible acceleration, but if you're a stop-light hero or drag-strip racer, you'll want everything you can get.

Every racer is looking for the "unfair advantage," some secret engine building ingredient that nobody else has found. In this instance the recipe is to go for absolute accuracy in every detail, and to make every part as light as is physically possible without sacrificing strength. It's often possible because the manufacturer didn't want to go to the trouble of extra machining. Then again, it may not have been desirable for an all-round street bike.

FORCED INDUCTION

There is another major area of performance engine improvement we haven't looked at yet: forced induction. Supercharging and turbocharging both come into this category — where the fuel/air mix is rammed into the motor by mechanical means. By increasing the amount of mix in the combustion chamber, the combustion pressure is increased, which can lead to large increases in horsepower.

Unfortunately, nothing comes for free, the payback in this instance is that large quantities of heat are also generated. One of the main enemies of engine life is detonation, which occurs when the combustion chamber temperature gets high enough to cause the fuel/air mix to burn before the spark has been triggered. This situation — where the temperature and pressure are out of control — produces an explosion instead of a nicely controlled burn. The shock waves generated can destroy all manner of engine components — piston rings may shatter, crowns may melt, sparkplug tips may disintegrate, and so on.

The way around this is to fit lower compression pistons, and some form of pressure relief valve in the intake system. This way the combustion pressure can be increased up to the safe level gaining extra horsepower, but because of the relief mechanism the motor will not self-destruct. There is really only one way to raise the intake pressure, and that is to fit a compressor of some sort. This can take any one of several forms: an impeller, sliding vanes, lobed rotors, etc. There are, however, only two basic ways to drive it. One is to drive it mechanically, via a belt, chain or gear-set; this is known as supercharging.

The second system is to utilize some of the energy left in the exhaust gas, by driving a fan with it. This has a drive shaft linked to the compressor so, as the exhaust pressure rises, the fan turns faster and faster, creating more and more compression in the intake. This is known as turbocharging.

ABOVE: If you want your motor to last, it's a good idea to be able to keep an eye on the oil pressure — this is the Ness-Tech oil pressure gauge and bracket assembly.

BELOW: If you want to go for maximum performance, you'll need to reduce the weight of everything, especially anything that rotates or reciprocates. This is the end of the crank; if you fit a belt primary you don't need the compensating mechanism, so you can mount a pulley directly without all that extra power-sapping weight.

TURBOCHARGING

On a turbocharger, a pressure relief valve is pre-set to divert the exhaust gas away from the fan (the proper name for it is an impeller). This device prevents too much compressing from taking place, and is known as a "wastegate." The normal boost level for a road bike would be around 5psi. This equates to about a quarter increase in horsepower, so a Harley tuned to produce 80bhp could be expected to reach 100bhp with a turbo.

There are many ways to increase this still further; in fact, turbocharging is almost a complete science unto itself. The simplest way to go faster is to increase the boost pressure, but going much above 5psi will require all sorts of precautions. One of these is to fit water injection, which sprays a fine mist into the intake manifold, having the effect of lowering combustion temperature. It also has the added bonus of increasing what's known as the "charge density." This simply means that more fuel/air mix gets into the motor each time, giving more power. When water injection is used, alcohol is sometimes mixed in with it to further improve matters.

There's another way to achieve the same thing, and that's to fit an intercooler, which is basically a radiator through which the fuel/air mix is passed. It lowers the mixture's temperature, increasing its density. Unfortunately, while it may work brilliantly, especially on trucks and drag cars, an intercooler is a big unit, usually way too big to fit neatly on a motorcycle.

At the college where I teach motorcycle engineering I'm often asked why turbos don't get used more often on bikes. Well, all the above problems make it difficult enough to start with, but there are more added complications. It's very difficult to get a good match between the parts that make up a turbo, and the engine to which it's being fitted. Every detail of both the exhaust side and the compressor side have an effect on its workings. If the exhaust fan and housing are too large, then there will be little increase in horsepower until way up in the rev range. Get the sizes too small, and there will be little overall improvement.

Another problem is to do with what's called "throttle lag." This means that when the throttle is opened, it takes a long time for the turbo to produce any boost. On the road this can translate into a bike that's really frustrating to ride, with the turbo taking too long to cut in to be a useful aid to overtaking or blasting between corners.

The single most important issue as far as the turbo is concerned is its oil supply. A turbo shaft can spin at enormous rpm. We're used to cranks spinning at up to 9,000rpm on a race-bike, but a turbo shaft may spin at 100,000rpm. No "normal" bearings will deal with this speed. Ball race bearings go into a condition called "skid" if they are run faster than the design speed. Needle rollers suffer from the same problem. Plain bearings are much better, but those fitted to turbos are a special type, called "floating" plain bearings. These require a film of oil on the outside as well as the inside, and they turn at half the speed of the shaft. This gives them a sort of "suspension," which damps out most of the nasty shock waves tearing around inside a turbo at such high revs.

So it can be seen that the bearing needs lubricant to survive, but the oil also has another function in a turbo: it acts as a coolant. If you see a turbo running on a test bed, you'll see that it glows bright red when it's working hard. Temperatures may well be around 1,500°F at the exhaust fan — and within an inch or so of this heat, we're expecting an oil-filled bearing to survive. This is another reason why a lot of speed is needed in the oil flow — if it stagnates, not only does the bearing stop working, but the oil will get cooked. Consequently, if the oil supply fails, the bearing will self-destruct very quickly. Not only is it very important to ensure that the oil can get to the turbo without any restrictions, it's also vital to make absolutely sure that it can get out again. If the oil "backs up" even for a small amount of time, the bearing will fail. When it does so, it usually takes the shaft with it, something that can cost several hundred dollars to fix.

This business of getting the oil out in a hurry means that, unless you fit an extract pump, the unit will need to be fitted higher than wherever the oil is going to return to — either the crankcase or the oil tank. My personal preference is to use a completely separate oiling system, and to use the best synthetic oil you can afford. This way you can ensure that absolutely no particles of worn engine can get into the turbine bearings, and you can provide extra pumps and coolers as necessary.

The bottom line is that unless you're buying a product that someone else has developed, fitting a turbo can lead to months of headaches and expense to get the engine running properly.

ABOVE and BELOW RIGHT: This ornate, radical Sportster called "Turned Loose" was built by Cory Ness and features a massive turbocharger. This forced induction system breathes through a twin-throat, sidedraft carburetor. As you can see, a turbocharger leaves little leg room when mounted like this. The sacrifice of riding comfort, however, is more than made up for in the dramatic increase in raw power — hence turbochargers are normally only seen on show customs or drag bikes. Note how both exhausts feed into the primary stage of the turbocharger and exit across the front of the motor.

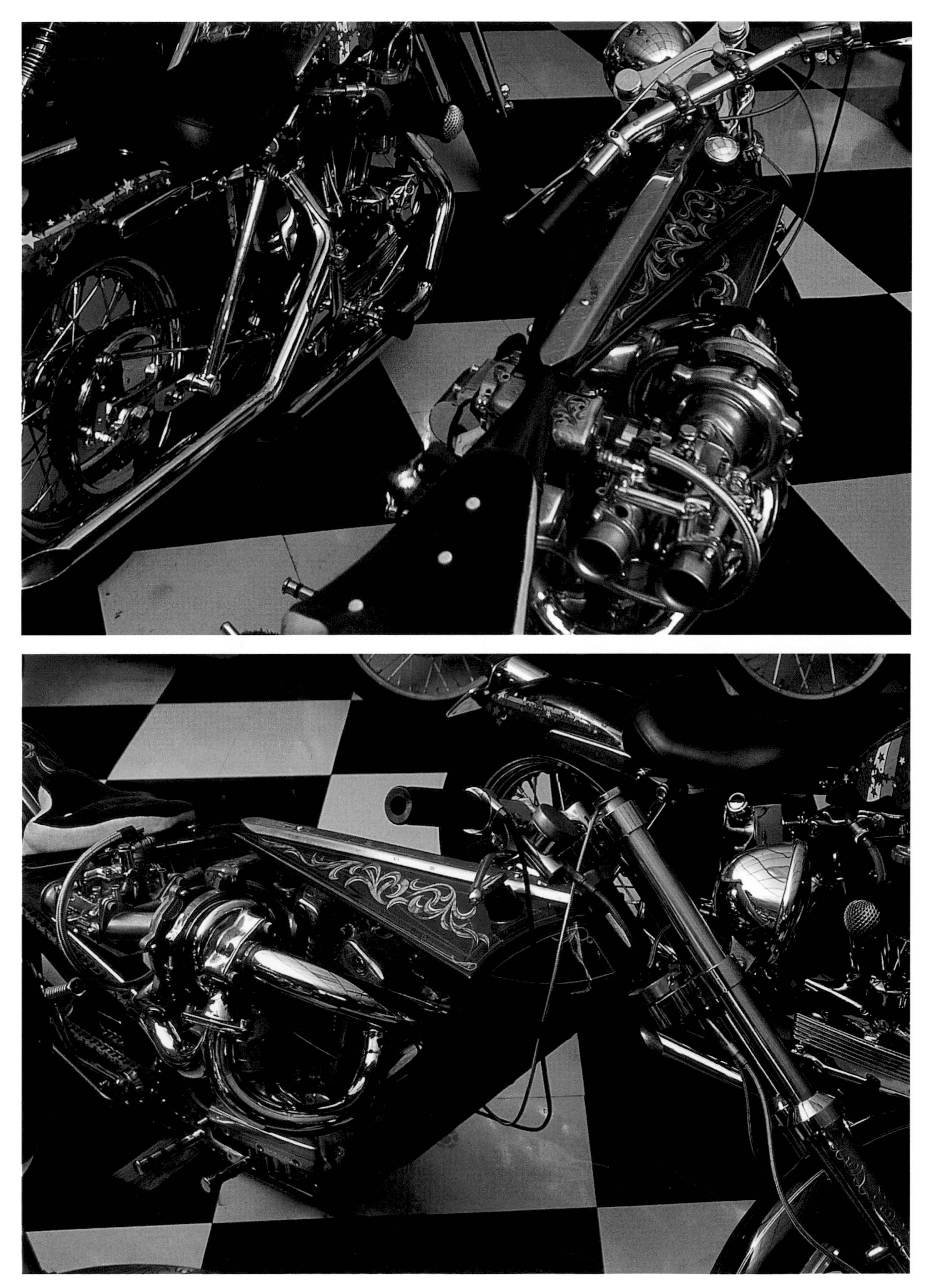

TOP: This gorgeous motor is fitted with a supercharger and a sidedraft twin throat carburetor . . .

ABOVE: Actually it's fitted with two superchargers, as can be seen from above.

BELOW: Getting the drive system right on a supercharger is often a hassle. Here's a close-up of one solution.

SUPERCHARGERS

These have been used on motorcycles for years — after the war some tuners discovered that the blowers used on bomber aircraft to increase cabin pressure were just the right size for a drag bike. They were usually mounted forward of the motor, and driven off the end of the crank via belts and pulleys. Sometimes there's room to mount one behind the motor if a stretched frame is being used.

All the problems experienced using turbos regarding heat also apply to superchargers, but they have some other unique problems as well — not least of these is that, because a supercharger is mechanically driven, it's driven all the time. This means it's driving when you want it to, but it's also driving when you're sitting at every set of stoplights. It doesn't take much traffic to make a supercharger a real liability, for it will overheat very quickly. The perfect answer is to fit some form of clutch into the drive system, so you can turn it off whenever you like.

I would hate to think that I have put anyone off forced induction, but what I am hoping to have illustrated is that these are subjects only for the very experienced.

NITROUS OXIDE INJECTION

While providing similar horsepower increases, nitrous oxide injection is perhaps a better route to go than turbos and superchargers. You may have heard of nitrous oxide before without realizing it — for years it's also been known as laughing gas, the stuff that anaesthetists used to use to knock people out!

The principle is very simple — nitrous oxide is a gas, which is released under pressure into the intake system. It carries a lot of oxygen in its chemical make-up, so when extra fuel is pumped into the motor as well, massive increases in horsepower can be achieved. It's very simple to fit a nitrous kit to a bike — it doesn't require low compression pistons for a start, so you don't have to go tearing the motor down to install it.

It also has the advantage that the system just sits there looking good and not getting in anyone's way until you want the extra horsepower. Most of the time, if another rider pulls up next to you at the stop-lights and sees the nitrous bottles, he'll decide to go in a different direction rather than race you. The bottles may be empty, but he isn't going to know that!

There are problems with nitrous though: it needs good quality valves to control the gas supply. Nitrous is cold when it is released into the motor, and the hose line temperature drops dramatically: this will freeze sub-standard quality valves very quickly. If they're

LEFT: Here's Big Al's bike again. A serious bike that demanded some serious horsepower. Nitrous oxide provided that bit extra . . .

BELOW: This where it comes from — the cylinder stores high pressure gas until needed.

BOTTOM: And this is where it goes — aircraft quality hosing is vital. It also helps to psych out the guy next to you at the stop-lights!

frozen, they won't shut off when required to do so, sometimes resulting in a substantial explosion. Such an explosion will at best do a lot of damage, and at worst it could be life threatening. Similar problems are caused if the extra fuel supply fails while the nitrous injection is in operation.

The message I'm trying to get across here is that if you want the large amounts of bolt-on horsepower nitrous oxide can supply, do it properly. Don't be afraid to spend money on high quality componentry, and find a supplier experienced at using it.

FUEL

If you're intent on going drag racing, you'll need to learn about special fuels. There are three basic types of fuel available for motorcycles — gasolines, alcohols, and nitromethane (which is very different from nitrous oxide). Only gasoline-based fuels are suitable for road use, as alcohol and nitro have all sorts of special requirements; for example, a motor will consume roughly three times as much alcohol as it will gasoline. Also they are both expensive, nitro being prohibitively so. One of the advantages of running alcohol is that it's a lot less sensitive to accurate jetting than gasoline. However, a drawback is that the entire system needs to be drained off every time it gets used.

These fuels are really for the more serious drag racer— bikes running nitromethane need to have the engine oil changed every time they run up the quarter -mile strip. That's *every* time, and some of the top guys even change the pistons as well! This is because nitro is extremely close to being liquid explosive, so the environment inside the motor is extreme. One of the byproducts of combustion when running is nitric acid, which finds its way past the piston rings and into the sump. Anyone who has used nitric acid knows that it is extremely corrosive to most things, especially metals — this is why the oil has to be changed so frequently.

IGNITION SYSTEMS

There are three main types of ignition system fitted to Harleys. These are contact breakers, magneto, and electronic. The simplest of these is the contact breaker system. All ignition systems work with the same overall principle: they have an ignition coil (also referred to as the high tension coil), some form of trigger assembly, and a power supply. The ignition coil features one or more high tension wires each with a sparkplug terminal. The spark itself is generated by the ignition coil, in a simple but clever manner. Although called a coil, it's really a high-speed transformer composed of two coils wound around a soft iron core. When the smaller of the two coils (called the primary), is connected to a 12V supply, it creates a magnetic field around itself. If the power is turned off, the magnetic field collapses — no surprise there.

However — and this is the clever bit — as the field collapses, it tries to turn itself back into electrical energy wherever it finds a turn of wire. This is where the other coil (called the secondary) comes in — it has a lot more turns than the primary, and therefore most of the energy gets converted here. The actual number of turns is roughly 200 on the primary and 20,000 on the secondary.

The actual amount of power generated for the spark depends on how quickly the magnetic field collapses, which is why a condenser is fitted across the contact breakers. The purpose of the condenser is to stop any arcing at the breakers, which would otherwise allow the primary to discharge slowly, greatly reducing the spark voltage. This is why a bike won't run properly if the condenser has failed — there isn't enough spark to ignite the fuel mix. Arcing across the breaker points also burns the contact surface away, meaning regular replacement would be required, so the condenser is actually performing two different jobs at the same time.

It's also worth noting that when the magnetic field in the ignition coil collapses, about 1/200th of the spark voltage is also generated in the primary coil. This equates to approximately 250V, which is "absorbed" by the condenser — if this didn't happen, the contact breaker faces would be eaten in short order.

A popular modification on Harleys is to convert the cylinder heads to allow twin sparkplugs. The idea behind this is to ignite the fuel/air mix from two sides at the same time. The thing about Harley motors that makes this a good idea is that, in having a large capacity but only two cylinders, the combustion chambers are inherently vast in comparison to a "multi." This means that it takes quite a long time for the combustion to get going, by which time the piston may well be past the point of doing any useful work. By starting the "burn" from two sides at once, theoretically the combustion event can be more efficient.

There is a side effect from this that is also beneficial — stock Evolutions have the wrist pin slightly offset, in order to stop the piston banging about in the cylinder, which causes engine noise. Minimizing engine noise in an air-cooled motor is a major problem for the Harley-Davidson factory, which has spent millions of dollars trying to bring their bikes within the noise limits imposed by legislation. This is fine for a stock road bike, but for those of us who like to build custom bikes it's an unnecessary source of friction, and hence power loss and overheating.

When a set of big bore cylinders is fitted to a motor, it will have performance pistons that will have the wrist pins in the true centerline — where they should be. These pistons will, however, rattle about in the bores more than the stockers, because the flame front created by a single sparkplug hits the piston crown at an angle. This knocks it over to one side,

ABOVE RIGHT: Ignition coils live behind the left-hand side panel on this Arlen Ness bike.

BELOW RIGHT: AMS billet twin-coil mount.

BELOW: Twin coils installed on a Shovelhead. If you're uprating your ignition, don't forget to fit high quality leads.

from where it will bounce backwards and forwards until the next combustion cycle. With two sparkplugs, however, the theory is that the pressure on the piston crown is symmetrical, causing a lot less bouncing, and therefore less noise, wear, and heat build-up.

Whether or not the twin-plug conversion makes any difference can be hard to prove — but it does look good! You'll need to fit an extra ignition coil, or replace the one you have with a dual-plug unit. This brings us neatly onto the subject of aftermarket coils, of which — like so many other components — there is a vast choice. You can purchase ones made by Accel, RevTech, Custom Chrome, etc. The high performance coils supply a much higher voltage to the sparkplug than the stock item, assisting starting, idling, and providing a smoother power curve.

Even if you decide not to fit a performance coil, it's worth considering fitting some custom sparkplug wires. These can provide much better insulation, and have higher quality conductors than stock, with a resulting increase in the voltage delivered to the sparkplug. Another plus is that there are many colors available, so you can choose a set to match your paint job!

IGNITION MODULE

One of the first things that most Harley owners do is to throw away the stock ignition module and fit an aftermarket performance item in its place. This is because the stocker has a rev limiter at 5,200rpm, and an advance curve designed to meet emissions' regulations, not to produce the best power output.

Yet again there are many to choose from: when buying, take care — these are expensive items, so don't go buying one that is unsuited to your bike. Some of those on the market allow the rider to choose different advance curves, and sometimes a different rev limiter setting. Alternatively you can buy a specific adjustable rev limiter module from Accel or Dyna.

Many owners choose to go for "single fire" ignition. This means that the stock system, which fires both sparkplugs at once, is replaced by one where the sparkplugs are fired individually. This allows each cylinder to run more independently, which smoothes the motor out, especially when the trouble is taken to ensure that the ignition timing is set accurately on each cylinder.

MAGNETO IGNITION

At the start of this section I mentioned magneto ignition. This used to be very popular because a good "mag" can produce a very high energy spark. Years ago contact breaker ignition systems could not produce the

ABOVE: Coil mounts come in many shapes and forms.

RIGHT: Ignition systems have progressed considerably since these bikes were new. Back then, magnetos were commonplace.

BELOW: Self-contained racing ignition system, by Interspan Ignition Co. This high energy unit only requires wires to the ignition trigger and the sparkplugs. It has internal batteries that can be recharged from an external source. It's light, simple, and highly effective.

voltages required for high performance applications, but magnetos could. These days electronic ignition is capable of delivering almost any spark energy we could possibly want, so mags are not as indispensable as they were previously. However, they do look nice, and they'll bring a lot of attention from admirers.

One of the attractions of a magneto is that it does not need a charging system or even a battery. This can simplify things, especially on a drag bike where you don't want to fit any unnecessary things like alternators. If you decide you like the idea of fitting one, Morris Magnetos can supply one, as can Karata Vertex.

INTAKES, CARBURETORS AND AIR CLEANERS

One of the most distinctive things about a Harley has always been the single carburetor sticking out of the right-hand side of the bike. Some riders find it gets in the way of their right knee — especially if the wrong forward-mounted footpeg is fitted. This is compounded if there is a large air cleaner as well.

In purely technical terms, the position of the carburetor should have been changed years ago, but Harley riders are a conservative lot. The factory has burned its fingers many times over the years trying to change things, but has found to its cost that changes were not popular and resulted in falling sales. There are many drawbacks to having the carb where it is, not least of which is that the whole assembly is vulnerable to damage if the bike goes down on its right-hand side. There is more to it than this though; the ideal situation for an air filter is to be able to draw in still air, so somewhere sheltered from wind-blast is a good starting point. Having the carburetor stuck out in the airstream gives rise to many potential problems — it's very hard to achieve accurate jetting because the air pressure is so variable.

Another problem with the stock layout is that, because of the difficulties mentioned above, the carburetor has to be mounted as close to the motor as possible. This means there is inadequate space to construct a proper intake manifold. Anybody who has played with Harleys for any length of time will know that this area is a source of trouble. There is so little room between the cylinder heads that it's very hard to ensure a perfect seal, and so air leaks are common. The Evolution rubber compliance fittings are a big improvement on what came before, but are still prone to leaks and age cracking.

The manifold designer has to try to ensure an even supply of fuel/air mix to both cylinders, but feeding two cylinders with an uneven firing angle makes this nigh on impossible. The perfect solution would be to fit two separate carburetors — just take a look at an XR750, an XR1000 or, if you have the budget for it, the VR1000 race-bike, which has two excellent intake manifolds, each fitted with a massive fuel injector.

RIGHT: This mind-blowing custom features a Ness-Tech billet air cleaner which contains a foam element for maximum filtration of intake air. Notice how its shape blends in very well with the overall style of the bike.

Air cleaners come in many styles:

LEFT: Round . . .

BELOW: Pancake (on twin 40mm IDF Webers) . . .

BELOW RIGHT: And none! This is a "velocity stack," also known as an intake "trumpet." It's the way to go for maximum air speed, but it won't filter anything this side of a two inch rock. It's fitted to an S&S "Shorty."

So the VR1000 has excellent intake manifolds does it? What makes them so good is their angle relative to the cylinder head. The bottom line with any engine is that its performance is ultimately limited to how much of the intake valve is working. If you take the stock Harley manifold and intake port, only about two-thirds of the valve is passing a useful amount of mixture. This is what cylinder head specialists are trying to improve when they perform gasflowing and porting.

When the intake tract is moved upwards from horizontal, the airstream approaches closer and closer to the line of the valve itself, meaning that more and more of its circumference gets used. This alone can result in a massive increase in horsepower. If you take a look at an Indy-car engine you will see exactly this arrangement, and for the same reasons the factory designed the VR1000 this way.

If you are building yourself a bike with serious performance in mind, give the above some thought. It's not easy to build a bike with vertical manifolds — for a start if you fit some carburetors that are going to do the new layout justice, you're not going to have room to fit a "normal" gas tank. My own way around this was to build a tank that wrapped around the back of the carbs; this was fine for a race bike, but it didn't allow for much fuel capacity.

TOP: A look straight down the throat of the beast! The Edelbrock heads on this bike have been modified to vent right into the carburetor, cleaning up the whole act.

ABOVE: This is the S&S air cleaner as fitted to thousands of Harleys.

TOP RIGHT: The Ness-Tech billet teardrop air filter complements this bike.

RIGHT: The SU has been a popular choice for many years; this is because it responds well to the large change in manifold pressure when the throttle is cracked open on a Harley. When finished as well as this one, they also look very pretty.

FAR RIGHT: This air cleaner has forward-facing inlets which will be beneficial if the mixture stays correct at speed, something that is hard to check accurately.

HARLEY-
DAVIDSON

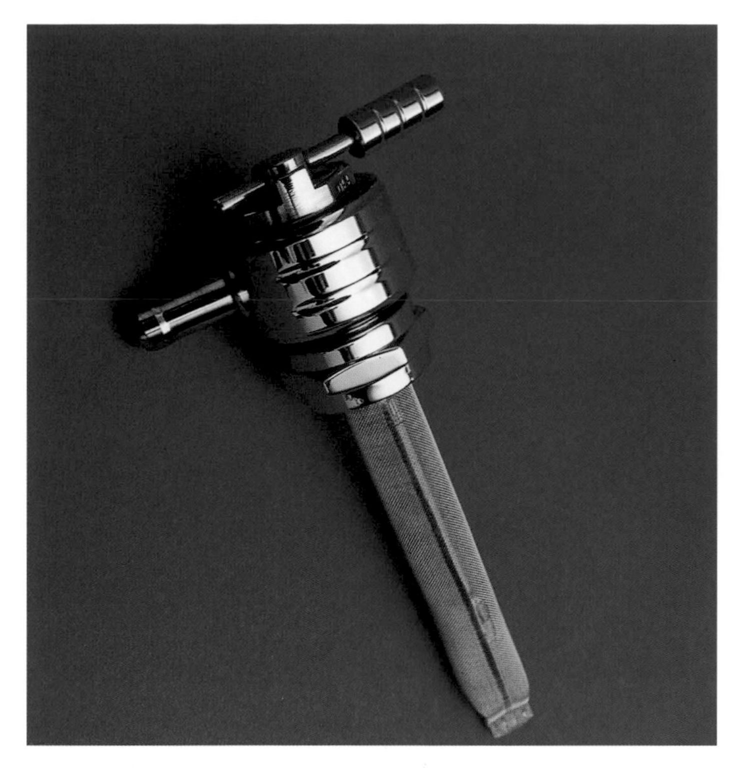

ABOVE: One of the first things to do when increasing the performance of a Harley is to fit a high flow petcock — the stock item can barely keep up with the standard motor! This is a Ness-Tech/Pingel Super-Flow gas valve.

BELOW LEFT: Typhoon performance carburetor by Carl's Speed Shop.

BELOW RIGHT: Twin-throat sidedraft carburetor with matching filter.

CARBURETORS

Harley riders are spoiled for choice when it comes to carburetors for stock-type manifolds — these are known as "sidedraft." If you want to fit vertical ones though, you'll be limited to "downdraft" types which are few and far between on motorcycles, so you'll need to go chasing automobile suppliers. I ended up using two Weber IDF twin throats, one for each cylinder — with four valve heads it means that I can get one throat per intake valve, so I have four manifolds! These were of the type originally designed to mount on a Ferrari.

If you decide to stick with stock-type sidedraft manifolding, then, as mentioned above, you have a huge array of carburetors from which to choose. Over the years probably every make has been tried on a Harley. Builders have tried single-throat, twin-throat, one on the right, one on each side, and even downdraft (on a sidedraft manifold!).

If you're serious, but broke, the stock Keihin slide carburetor fitted to some Evolutions can be made to work very well, with modifications such as an Andrews Accelerator Pump Kit, larger jets, and a free flow air cleaner. If your model doesn't have one of these fitted, they can be picked up cheaply at swap meets.

A replacement carburetor is the way most riders choose to go — the list of suppliers and models is extensive. These include Harley's own "Screaming Eagle" that works very well; some other suppliers are Mikuni, Zenith, RevTech, S&S, and Keihin. All the time newer and bigger designs are being produced by aftermarket manufacturers. For years the S&S "Super" series were the way to go — these were produced in a variety of sizes, from small models to bucket-sized ones for top-fuel drag bikes. Over the years I've used S&S carbs myself with excellent results.

One of the modifications that can be made to some Harley carburetors is an adjustable main jet. This makes it very easy to experiment with different mixture settings — it is even possible to alter the main jet size while the engine is running. This is a feature that many riders of "other" makes are very envious of. For most of them a change in jet size requires some serious spanner work, as well as a reach into the wallet. Adjustable main jets are available for S&S, Zenith, and Keihin carburetors.

Another aftermarket part is the "Thunderjet," which allows the tuner to add another fuel circuit, facilitating more accurate jetting at mid and high revs. The "Thunderjet" is available to fit S and S, Keihin,

ABOVE: Beautiful Panhead with stock cleaner.

BELOW LEFT: SU with domed grille cleaner.

BELOW RIGHT: S&S air cleaner element on a Shorty carburetor.

ABOVE: This Shovelhead motor has an S&S carburetor with an unidentified (home-made?) air cleaner.

BELOW and ABOVE RIGHT: The air cleaner (detail BELOW) on this bike is unmistakably an Arlen Ness billet creation!

BELOW RIGHT: This RMD drag bike uses an open velocity stack on a large S&S carburetor.

FAR RIGHT: Ness-Tech billet "Air Scoop."

and Zenith carburetors. It looks good, and in my experience, works well.

There is also the "Yost Power Tube," which is a kit comprising a high performance emulsion tube, throttle needle and some new jets. It's claimed to assist combustion, and that it cleans up the carburation and improves acceleration; however, I haven't had the opportunity to use one yet myself so I don't know whether it does everything claimed.

AIR CLEANERS

Having looked at carburetors, I now want to examine air cleaners. As with many other Harley parts, there is a vast choice of these on the market — from simple "pancake" types through to elaborate billet examples. Some work better than others, but most are sold because the purchaser likes the look of them. When selecting one for your ride, there are various features to look out for. An air cleaner's most important function is, of course, to filter out airborne particles. The vast majority of dust picked up by an engine is made up of minute quartz fragments, which are essentially similar to grinding paste — need I say more?

It is also important that an air cleaner should not restrict the airflow too much, or else it's going to cost you horsepower. The problem is that if the filter is going to keep debris out of your motor — and be free flowing at the same time — it needs to have a large surface area. This means it's going to be big, but unfortunately big air cleaners don't look very nice, so somewhere there might have to be a compromise.

There is an extensive choice of air cleaners on the market — there are shapes from teardrop to round, from wedge to domed. They can be made of chromed steel sheet or mesh, and of cast or billet aluminum. Whatever external shape they are, it's the internal shape that really counts to the motor; that and the construction of the cleaner element itself. You can purchase these separately if you wish; they come in two basic types, disposable (usually made of paper) and cleanable (usually made of some kind of foam). One of the biggest suppliers of elements is K & N, who also supply a variety of other related things like filter oil.

MOUNTING BRACKET

When purchasing a new carburetor, it's easy to overlook the mounting bracket that holds it in place. If this is neglected the compliance fittings will soon fail, causing air leaks and subsequent poor running. There are several different bracket types to choose from, so you'll have to decide which fits your application and which you like the look of.

RMD
S&S
PERFORMANCE
CARBURETORS
Cycle

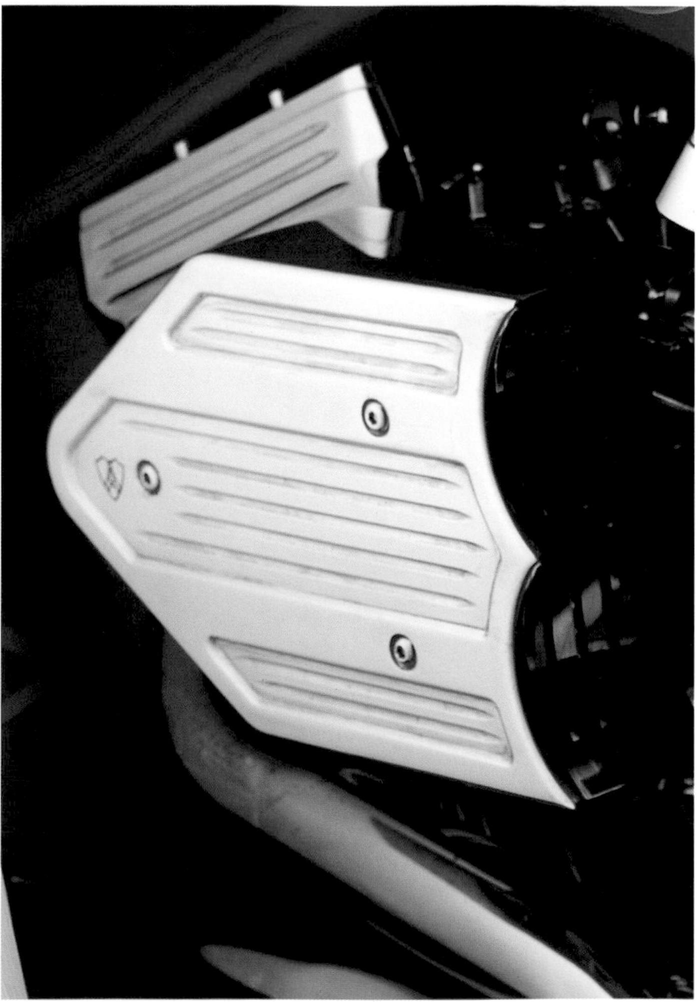

PRIMARY DRIVE AND TRANSMISSION

When we come to look at the primary drive and transmission, we meet the most fundamental difference between Sportsters and Big Twins — the engine is integral with the tranny on Sporties, but separate on the big ones. Each system has its strengths and its pitfalls. For instance, you're stuck with the original tranny on a Sportster, but on the Big Twin you can fit anything you like. If you're into drag racing, you may want to do something a little bit different — maybe fit a lighter unit, as the stock layout is very heavy.

In the 1970s, during the bad old days of AMF ownership, Harley transmissions got a pretty bad reputation for unreliability, particularly with the Sportsters. These days things are much improved. They are inherently strong, but there are still many aftermarket parts to upgrade them. Basically there are two major types — four- and five-speed. You can build an entire unit for a Big Twin without a single factory component, with parts available from a number of different manufacturers. Andrews supply close ratio gear clusters which were initially developed for drag strip use, although these days they're used on road bikes everywhere. They are constructed from high grade nickel alloy steel and then heat-treated, giving them strength and durability. A similar product is offered by RevTech.

Aftermarket transmission cases are manufactured by STD from heat-treated "356 T6" aluminum alloy. This is a high quality material, which — when matched with extra thick castings — makes a very strong replacement for the stock item.

RIGHT: When a chain snaps it can cause severe injury to the rider or pillion if it is left unguarded. It can also cause the bike to go out of control if the chain locks the rear wheel. The billet chain guard fitted to this bike provides form and function in one unit.

BELOW: The transmission in all its glory! This is a stock Harley gear cluster with Arlen Ness cases.

CHAINS

The primary chaincase is an area we have yet to examine. The primary serves to transmit the rotation of the crankshaft to the gearbox via a chain. In so doing it passes through the clutch. On the end of the crank is a device designed to act as a sort of shock absorber — it takes out a lot of the mechanical pulses which could otherwise damage the transmission, and in so doing also smoothes out the feel to the rider. This device is known as the compensating mechanism.

While chains are a good thing from the manufacturer's point of view — they're cheap and reasonably trouble free — they can be improved on. If you decide to stay with a chain drive, probably the biggest improvement you can make is to fit a quality aftermarket tensioning system. This will lessen the amount of slack in the primary, giving a smoother ride. It'll also help to quiet the chain down and make it last longer in the bargain.

BELT DRIVE

A lot of companies offer belt primary drive conversions — which should not be confused with secondary belt drives linking the gearbox to the rear wheel.

A belt has a certain amount of inherent shock-absorbing qualities, which means that for a hot rod or drag bike the compensator can be removed. They're much lighter than a chain and a lot quieter. They also don't waste as much horsepower as a chain (less friction). Once set up correctly, they require less maintenance. There is a downside (isn't there always?). Belt drives don't like debris getting caught up in them, especially the sort of small rocks often thrown up from the road. So, if you're going to fit a belt drive, make sure that there's an adequate cover or guard.

CLUTCH

There have been many different clutches fitted to Harley Big Twins over the years, some better than others. There are many ways that a clutch can be improved — depending on what the bike is going to be used for. Most road applications will benefit from a decent set of aftermarket clutch plates, such as those made by Barnett.

An area where particular performance gains can be made is the primary — it's possible to get rid of a lot of heavy rotating components, and replace them with lightweight performance items — things like the compensating mechanism, the generator rotor (don't take this off if you still want a charging system!), the primary chain, the crank sprocket, and the entire clutch assembly. If you want to lighten things still further, the primary cases themselves can go. You'll need to fit a special bearing support plate behind the clutch if you do this, though.

If you decide to replace the clutch, there are several on offer from performance specialists. As mentioned earlier, Barnett is one of the big names in clutches. A good unit will not only improve quarter mile times, but will also improve gearshifting.

Talking of clutches, there are several ways to improve the action at the lever. One of these is to convert the lifting mechanism from a mechanical unit to a hydraulic one. To do this a handlebar master cylinder is fitted in place of the original clutch lever. If this unit matches the brake master cylinder it can look really good. It will smooth up the operation of the clutch, and make it lighter as well. For those who don't have full strength in their left hand this may be a great help.

Another way of reducing the lever effort without going to the extent of a hydraulic system is to fit the White Bros. "Easyboy" Lite Clutch unit, which is still cable-operated, as before.

ABOVE LEFT: This belt primary drive looks good and is a neat installation. A polished guard protects the rider's leg from the moving belt. Belts are inherently quiet and smooth running.

BELOW LEFT: A chain primary drive seems primitive in comparison.

BELOW and BOTTOM: Two different hydraulic clutch master cylinders.

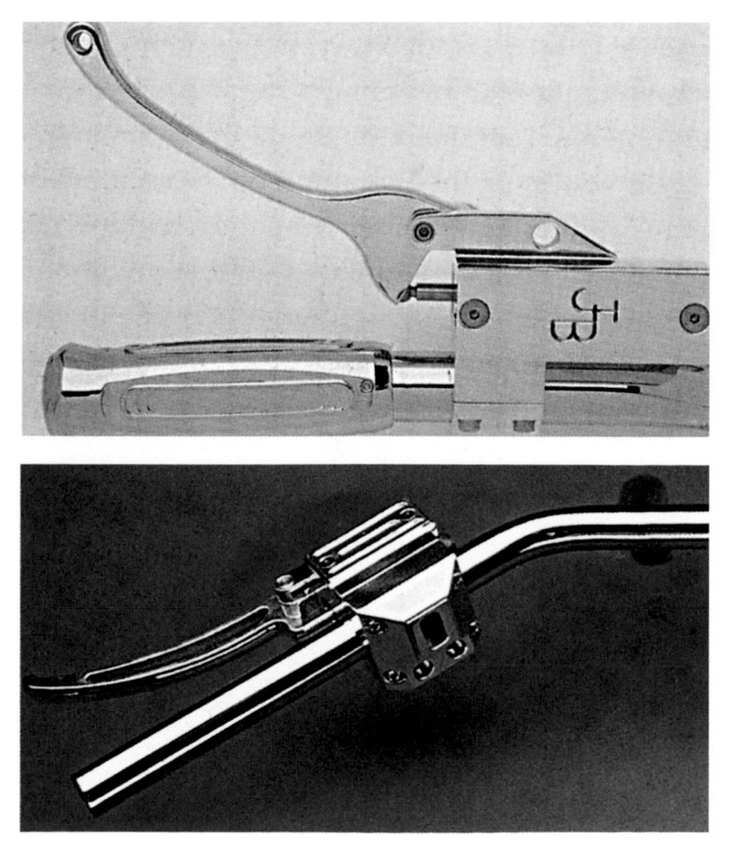

FRAMES AND TRIPLE TREES

When building any kind of motorcycle, be it a custom or not, the frame is the backbone of the project, from which everything else is derived. So let's take a look at what's involved.

The many types of frame used on Harleys can be loosely divided into two camps: those with and without rear suspension. Those without are known as "rigids"; those with rear suspension include twin shock, monoshock, plunger, sprung hub and Softtail.

When you've decided what type of Harley you're going to build, you may find you need to alter the frame to achieve your aim. Before any frame modifications are made, it's important to understand that bad changes can make a motorcycle dangerous. Some of these changes will make themselves felt at low speed, but others will only show up at much higher speeds, meaning that injury could result.

FRAME

Its most basic function is to hold the engine in place, and to hold the wheels together. However, the distances and angles between the various components can be absolutely critical. It's also important to understand that a lot of these will change as varying weights are placed on the motorcycle — I'm talking here about the rider/passenger and any luggage being carried. It's not unknown for a bike to be safe to ride solo, but unsafe two-up.

What are the critical dimensions then? Well, the most important ones are the fork angle (sometimes called the "rake"), the trail, and the wheelbase. There are many others that will have an effect, but most of these will only be of interest to a racer. The fork angle is simply that — the angle of the forks, measured from the vertical. A normal figure for a Harley would be in the region of 30° — however, the angle could be anywhere from 24° on a serious racing bike to 38° on a radical chop.

BELOW LEFT: Close-up of headstock molding before paint is applied.

BELOW: As mentioned earlier, neck molding needs to be kept to a minimum thickness or else it will eventually crack and fall out.

RIGHT ABOVE: Arlen Ness Softail frame for "Dark Angel," in primer . . .

RIGHT CENTER: . . . and painted.

BELOW RIGHT: Another Ness Softail frame, with minor differences to that of "Dark Angel." This time the frame is for a bike called "Paint It Black."

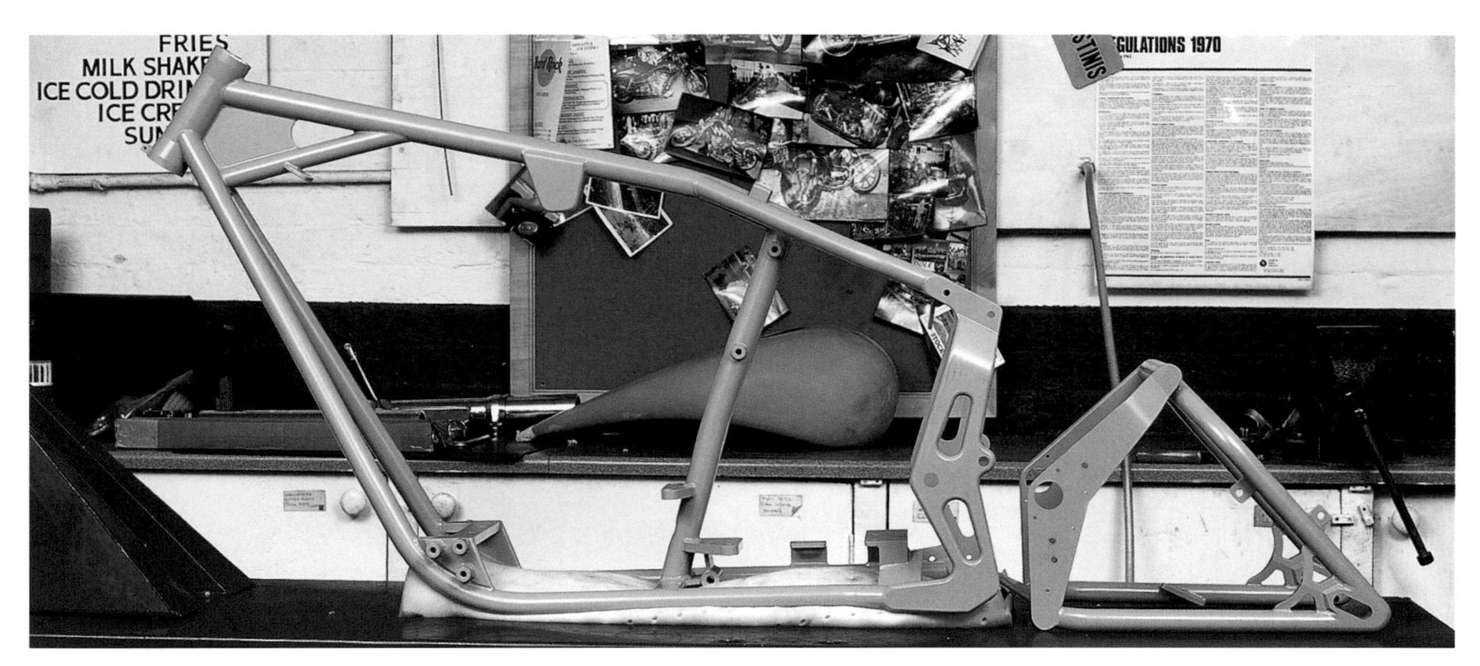
FRIES
MILK SHAK
ICE COLD DRI
GULATIONS 1970

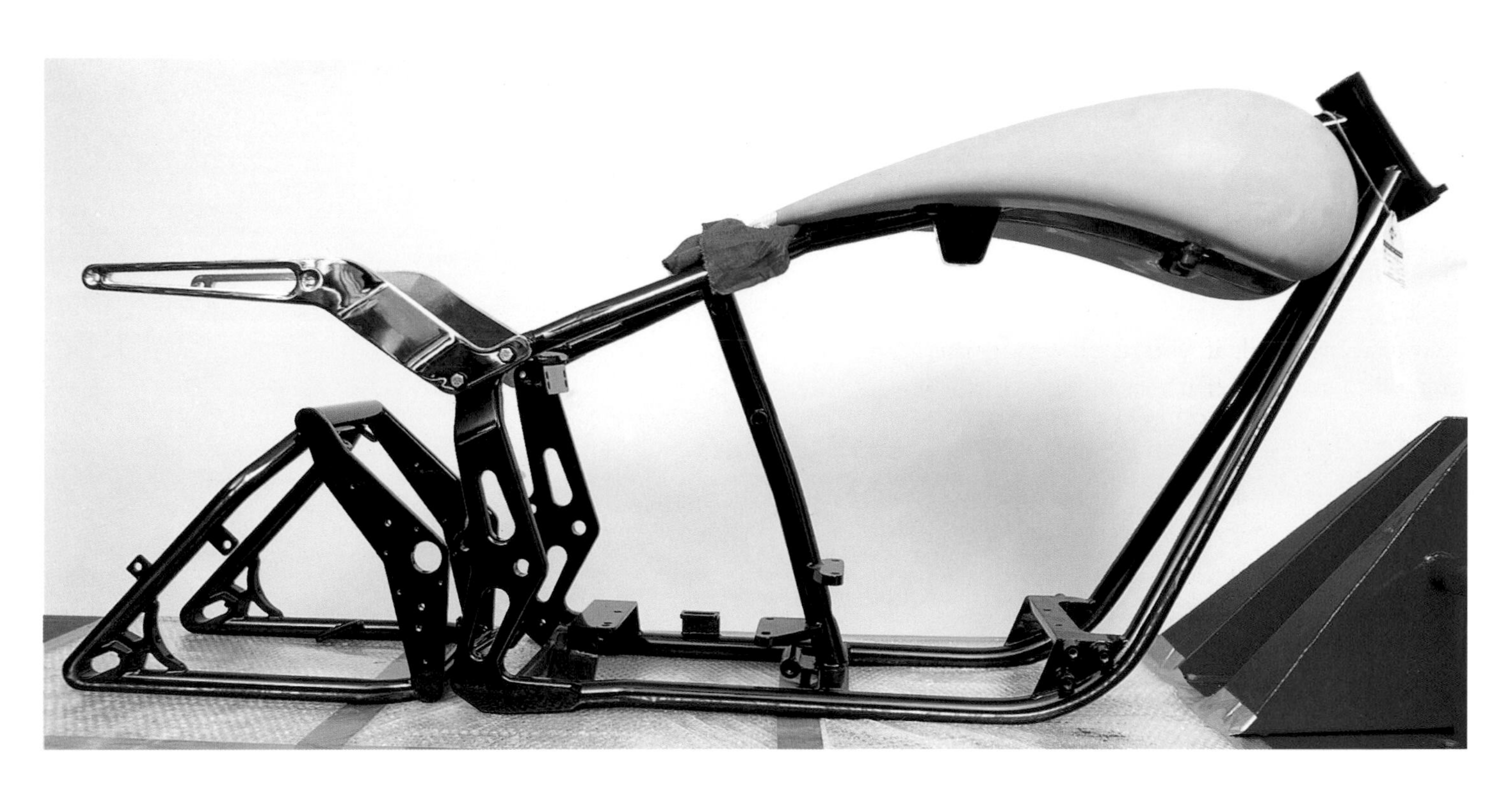

ABOVE: Here's "Dark Angel's" frame with gas tank (in primer) and fender struts fitted. From this point on, the build process should be just that — you should have decided on the angles for the fenders and gas tank early on in the design of the bike. Double-check at the dry build stage so that any changes necessary can be made before the application of any paint. When a component is delivered late, or has to be changed for some reason, it can be a real pain from now on.

The wheelbase is easy to understand — it's the distance measured between the front and rear wheel axles. If the distance is too great the bike will be hard to steer but very stable — ideal for long distance cruisers, but awful for canyon racers. The reverse is true for shorter wheelbases, the difference being that if the figure is too small, the bike can get unstable. Fortunately, if you're using a Harley motor, its length makes it almost impossible to shorten the wheelbase too much. The critical number is around 55in, depending upon a whole host of other factors, the most important of which is weight distribution.

The trail is the hardest one to check. If you draw a straight line down from your head stem, it will touch the ground a few inches ahead of the where the front tire contacts the ground. This figure is the trail, and should be anywhere from 3.5in (serious racing bike)

ABOVE: The front end of an Arlen Ness project bike, showing clearly the relationship between the headstock and the front axle. If you draw a line from the steering stem to the ground, you can see that there are about four inches from here to the center of the tire contact patch. This distance is called the "trail," and has a major effect on the way the bike will handle.

RIGHT: Detail of rubber engine mounts on Graham Duffy's AMS bike. This is a nice neat installation which looks good and works well.

to 5in (radical chop). The lower the figure, the less stable the bike will be. Too low and the bike may shake its head over bumps or get dangerous under braking. Conversely, if the figure is too high the bike will need a rider with the arms of a gorilla, and will be dreadful in corners.

So what can influence these figures when a bike is being built? Well, if you're changing the frame, find out who made it. If it's from one of the well-known and respected suppliers, you shouldn't have a problem. If, however, you are constructing one yourself or, worse, someone else is doing it for you, be very careful. Why do I say this? Well, you can be sure that the builder is very unlikely to ride it, so why will he care if it gets unstable in bumpy corners? If you're doing it yourself you will be (I hope) much more careful.

Frames are usually constructed of steel of various types. The best ones are made of TIG-welded chrome-moly, which is a material derived from the aircraft industry. Cold drawn steel is also excellent. Both of these are supplied as seamless tubing, which means there's no join in the tubing which could weaken it. Stock frames are made with the seamed stuff and then MIG-welded — but they're being mass-produced, so we'd expect nothing less.

The factory VR1000 race-bike has its frame constructed from aluminum, which has the advantage, when designed properly, of being light and stiff. Aluminum can also be used as an extrusion, or as seamless tube.

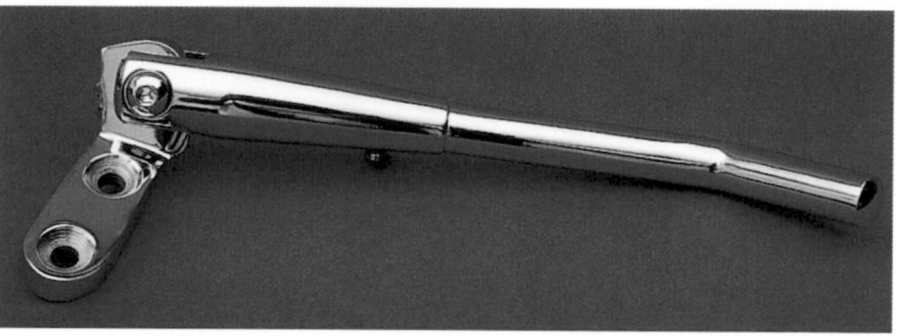

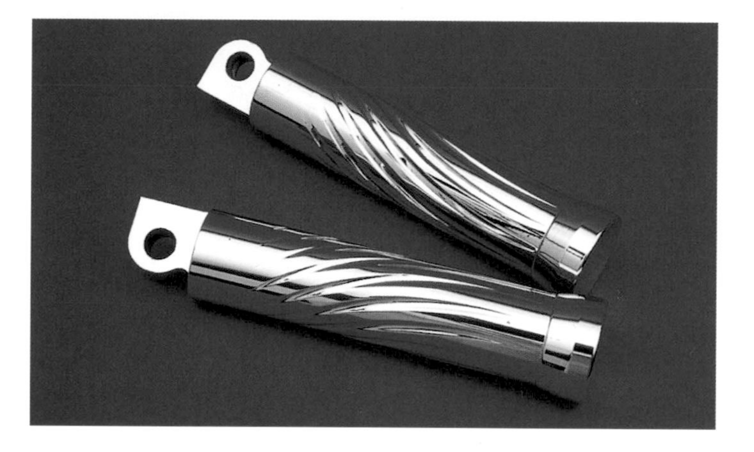

ABOVE TOP: A close-up of the headstock shows the horizontal bracing strut which stiffens the frame under braking. Notice also the bracing plate which reinforces the welded joints.

ABOVE CENTER: Road bikes need kickstands. This is a Ness item with mounting bracket.

ABOVE: Ness-Tech chromed billet aluminum "Twister" footpegs.

LEFT: The frame used on Graham Duffy's AMS bike was made from TIG- welded chrome-moly seamless tube by Planet Engineering. This is how most good custom bike frames are constructed. The headstock bracing plate is shaped to match in with the style of the rest of the bike. This is the sort of detail touch that makes the professionals stand out from the crowd.

ABOVE: Lightweight triple trees not only help to lower the overall mass of the bike, but also help to change direction quickly. This is of little interest to the boulevard cruiser, but vital to a racer. In this picture the lower tree is made of magnesium, which is the lightest material for the job. Maybe one day we'll be able to purchase composite triple trees made of carbon and boron fiber, but until then this is the best available.

BELOW: These stunning AMS Wide-Glide triple trees are made of CNC billet aluminum, and feature lightening recesses.

RIGHT: The triple trees on Dave Stewart's trike are also billet CNC, but they look quite different.

OPPOSITE PAGE: As you can see, just because triple trees are made of CNC billet aluminum, they don't all have to look the same: there's a wide range to choose from.

TRIPLE TREES

The parts that have more influence than any other over the bike's stability are the triple trees. The important dimension here is the distance between the steering stem and a line drawn between the center of the forks. Raising the offset lowers the trail, in other words the more offset, the less stable the bike will be. It is very important to match the offset to the length of the forks — and with the current fashion for short forks, it's more important than ever to do this. In the old days of enormous front ends it was nigh on impossible to make the trail too small.

One of the most popular modifications made to the front end is to change the triple trees for some custom ones. There are two basic materials used for their construction — steel and aluminum — but three if you count magnesium, which is only used on a few racing bikes.

A good set of custom trees looks great, cleaning up the front end, and often being made with extra width to allow a wide front wheel with twin discs. Most manufacturers will supply full kits, including triple trees, front wheel axle, disc spacers, wheel spacers, etc.

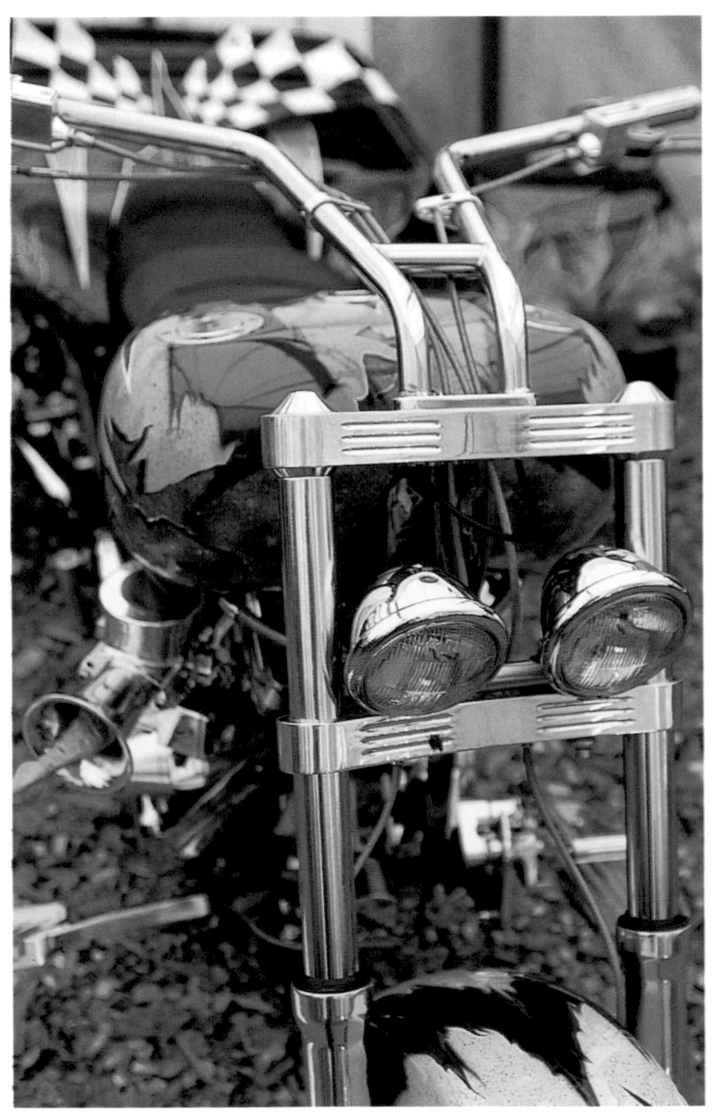

LEFT and RIGHT: Well-designed triple trees have to take into consideration the routing of wires from the headlight and brake hoses. Those illustrated have clearly been thought out very carefully.

FAR RIGHT: It's important to get the handlebar mounting right. If you use rubber anti-vibration dampeners and then fit high 'bars, you're going to end up with a lot of free play which will give the bike a very loose feel. Polyurethane is harder but still works well. Choosing the shape of your handlebars can make or break the look of the bike, so take your time to get it right. Getting the rise right is obviously just as important.

BELOW: Not all customs flaunt their triple trees. On this Arlen Ness creation — Ness-Stalgia — you can hardly see them in this side-view.

EXHAUSTS

One of the greatest pleasures of owning a Harley is the sound it makes. There's no equal to winding the throttle open in high gear and hearing the motor snarl at the world — that is, unless you've got a stock exhaust system, in which case the sound is best left undescribed. Depending on the local state laws, you may or may not stay legal if you modify your pipes — and this is something you must consider carefully. Some of the units fitted by the factory can be improved by applying a long metal bar and a big hammer — simply by knocking out the baffle plates. This'll improve the sound and throttle response, but remember that you'll almost certainly have to re-jet the carburetor because the factory sends its bikes out with very lean settings because of the emission laws. Whenever any changes are made to the exhausts, you must check the jetting or risk engine damage.

There are many sets of pipes on the market, some good and some bad. There are various factors to consider when choosing what to buy. First, it's worth making sure they'll be practical. Will they fit? Check the routing of the header pipes — do they clear the frame tubes? How about the timing cover? Consider the foot controls you're using — will the pipes clear them and any movement of the brake lever? Check everything before you part with cash.

The next issue to address is that of ground clearance. It never ceases to amaze me how low some people will mount exhausts on their bikes, knowing how restrictive they are. I know I mostly build race bikes, but I build show customs as well — and I like to ride them hard, so I won't accept low pipes. You can make up your own mind how far you want to lean your bike.

Talking of performance, if you've built yourself a hot rod and have taken the trouble to fit single-fire ignition and separate carburetors, then think about matching the pipe lengths. If not, then don't bother. Making sure the pipes are the same length helps the cylinders to run the same, which will increase horsepower and reduce vibration. Overall length counts too,

BELOW: What could be more classic than the upswept fishtails on this Panhead?

RIGHT: In fact they're so nice, we'll take a real close look at them!

DSK

but it's more important they don't set your leg on fire than if they'll produce another tenth of a horsepower!

When you look at all the different pipes, you also want to ask yourself what you want them to be made of. The usual choices are chromed steel, high temperature paint or stainless steel. For racing use there is titanium but this could end up costing more than you care to think of. I made mine, but finding titanium tubing is no easy matter. As I've mentioned elsewhere, stainless steel lasts a long, long time. Chrome-plated exhausts look good, but the finish will eventually either peel and fall off — or if you clean your bike often enough, you'll polish right through it.

The last and often the most important factor is whether you like the look of the pipes. If you don't like them — don't buy them. The definition of customizing is that you are personalizing your bike — so build it the way you want it to look. The exhaust system has a huge effect on the look and feel of a bike, so choose carefully.

TOP LEFT: Race-bike exhausts don't have to look nice, they just have to work well. These are made of seamless titanium, with aluminum mufflers. The springs are to allow quick removal, and to deal with the high levels of vibration that would fracture a solid mount.

ABOVE: The straight-through shotgun pipes look great as fitted to this Shovelhead, but are unlikely to impress the local law enforcement agency!

TOP CENTER: Leg guards are there for a purpose on this Sportster — you don't look cool if your leg's on fire!

TOP RIGHT: This Sportster has a two into one set-up, which can work well.

BOTTOM RIGHT: Ness-Tech/Bub Upsweeps combine traditional styling with modern performance and construction techniques.

Harley
Davidson

Crafts

ABOVE: Graham Duffy has chosen to keep his pipes short and simple, but has machined up some very nice billet end caps and support clamps to finish them off nicely.

ABOVE LEFT: Flare-Tip "Chopper" pipes on this Arlen Ness bike look wild, but help make the bike's styling look complete.

BELOW LEFT: Black pipes can look really good, as evidenced on yet another Ness bike.

RIGHT: Routing exhausts in behind bodywork looks great, but can be a real pain, as the heat generated can discolor paintwork, or in severe cases set fire to the bike — so take care!

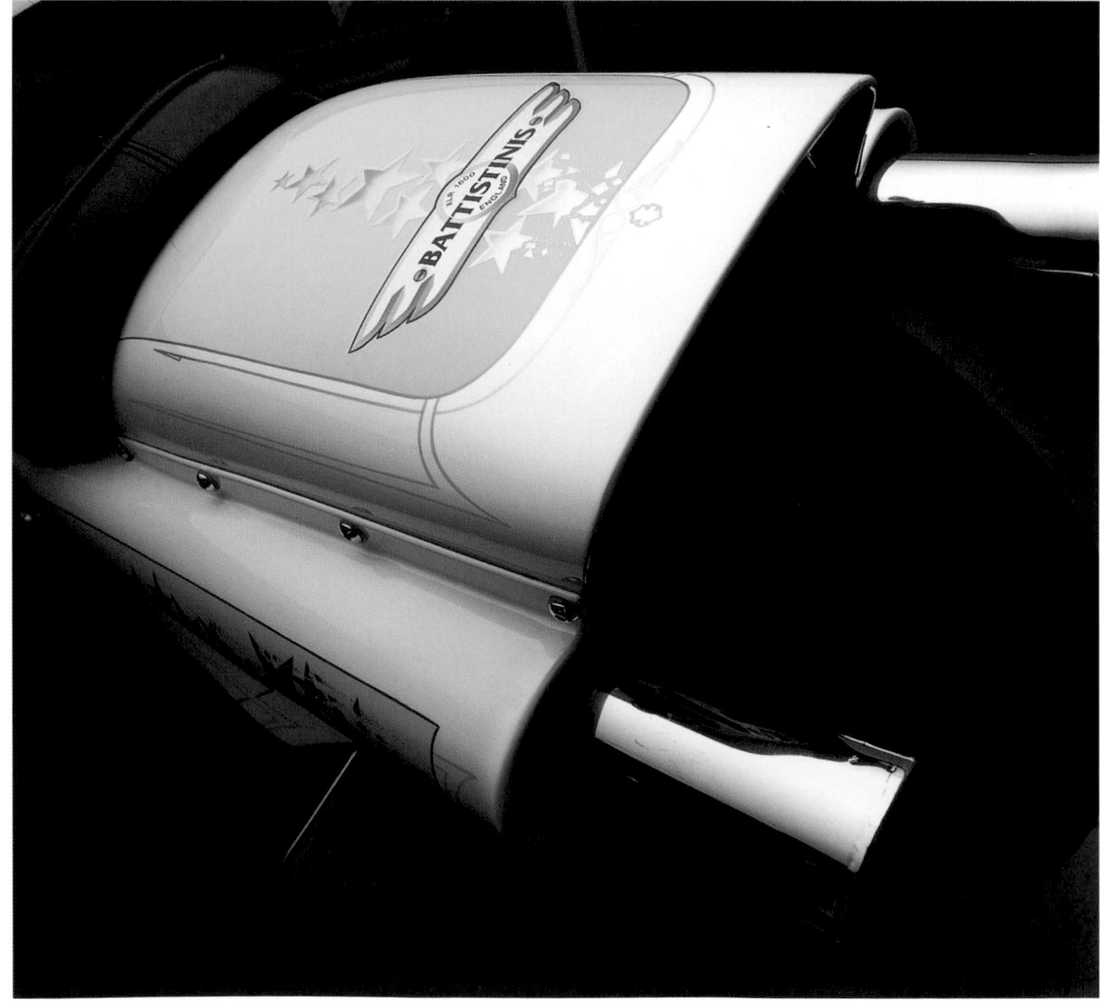

ABOVE: Here's a close-up of Graham Duffy's billet aluminum end caps on the AMS bike.

LEFT: And this is where those exhausts shown on page 77 exit the bodywork. They look great, and in the bargain look quite different from other customs, something which is hard to do these days. The bike is called "Showstar" and was built by Battistinis.

RIGHT: Getting the pipe lengths the same is important if you want your motor to run sweet. When you fit a two-into-one, it's even more important. The problem is that the rear cylinder is nearer the back of the bike than the front one, so the pipes are inherently different lengths. One answer is to lengthen the rear exhaust by running it forwards, and then back again, as seen here on this hot-rod Sportster.

Harley
Davidson

FINISHING

Nothing sets a bike apart more than its finish, be it paint, plate, or polish. As a component has to be polished before it can be plated, we'll take a look at what's involved in this process first.

To begin with, machine polishing is very different from running a waxed rag over your bike. Before a part can be polished it has to be thoroughly cleaned. This may involve chemically stripping paint off in a caustic bath, or it may be performed using some form of blasting treatment. If the component is delicate, then the blasting medium may be something soft like ground walnut shells. If the opposite is true, then something really abrasive like alumina could be used.

It is really important that engine parts *never* get blasted on the inside — the same is true of oil tanks. I have seen completely rebuilt engines destroyed in less than 500 miles through contamination with blasting grit. If the blasting shop assures you that a good wash will dislodge any particles, take your work elsewhere. Whatever promises they make, do any masking yourself — tape will be destroyed in seconds, so use metal blanking plates wherever possible.

When grit is fired at high speed towards anything made of aluminum (steel is not as sensitive), it gets trapped in the outer layers. Think of the metal as being made of a honeycomb, and it's easier to imagine. When the part gets washed, the grit stays right where it is; it will only come out when the metal gets hot and relaxes its grip on it. Unfortunately this condition is exactly what happens when the engine is running. It's also a gradual process, so the part may not be completely grit-free for thousands of miles. By then it's too late. Take this advice very seriously.

BELOW: Painting the motor black can save a lot of time polishing, but getting an even highlight on the cylinder fins will test your patience!

ABOVE: This Ness bike displays professional finishing in its highest form — not a flaw anywhere, be it in paint, plate, or polish. Be prepared either to spend a lot of time or a lot of money if you want a finish like this. Texture is very important when you're considering how to finish a component. Too much chrome, for instance, will detract from the overall impact of the bike. Tasteful use of polished parts blended with plated ones look much better.

SPINDLE POLISHING

If you've never seen an industrial spindle polisher being used before, you'll be amazed to watch the process. The machine looks like a bench grinder that stands about 3ft tall — instead of grinding wheels it has a cloth polishing "mop" at each end. These mops are coated with a special compound called "soap." This is done by holding a bar of soap up against the mop while it's spinning. These soaps come in many different compounds and grades, each one specific to a particular material. Most things can be polished, from metal to glass — even wood and some plastics — but it makes no sense to polish certain things, for instance magnesium or lead will oxidize back to being dull in minutes. It's also a waste of time getting a mirror finish on something that's going to be painted. In fact, as we'll see in the section on paint, it's important to get a good "key" for painted parts.

Once the mop has been loaded with soap, the polishing can begin. Depending on the mop's speed, and the shape of the component, great care may have to be taken not to damage the part or injure the operator. An industrial machine will have a lot of torque behind it and will be quite capable of wrenching something out of the operator's hands and throwing it across the shop floor. This will clearly not do the part, or the operator's temper, any good at all.

Getting a good consistent finish is something that takes a lot of practice — it's only too easy to end up with ripples right in the middle of a critical surface. If you're going to have a go yourself, start with some parts that don't matter too much, ideally some that won't get used on your bike at all. As the part goes through the polishing process the mops are changed; for instance, the one used for the initial work is described as a "cutting" mop. The last ones are called "finishing" mops.

PLATING

If the component is to be plated, don't forget that any ripples or marks will show right through — polishing is one of the things that separates the really good platers from the also-rans. There are many different types of plating, so let's take a quick look at them. First the component is polished and then it's hung in a special bath of chemicals, whereupon an electrical current is passed through it. While this is happening microscopic particles of the plating metal are deposited on the surface of the component. The time it takes varies with the depth of plate desired, and various other factors such as voltage and temperature. The best-known type of plating is, of course, chrome but before this a layer of nickel is deposited first. Sometimes the part will have a layer of copper plate applied before this. Every plater has his own tricks of the trade, for it's one of the great "black arts."

If you're planning to chrome-plate highly stressed components, such as a set of spokes — don't. When a part is chromed it also undergoes something called "hydrogen embrittlement," which can result in its premature failure. The only way to deal with this is to bake the part concerned in an oven. Even if you have access to an oven, think twice before attempting this yourself. If you do not want to go ahead, find a metallurgist to get specialist advice on temperatures and duration. If you live miles from an industrial city and can't find a metallurgist try searching the internet for help.

There are many other types of plating including cadmium, zinc, silver, gold, platinum, etc. Cadmium is a common original finish on nuts and bolts, so to the restorer it's worth knowing about, but it's not of much interest to the custom builder. The other plating materials are obviously decorative and expensive. If you decide to go for something like gold-plate, remember that the layer will be extremely thin; only use the polish the plater recommends.

Anodizing is a process used on aluminum only. It uses electrical current to penetrate the surface of the metal with a chemical dye. It's not a plating process as such, but one that can be used for protective purposes, such as the lovely red and blue oil line fittings made for aerospace and motor racing use. There is another type called "hard anodizing." This usually provides a clear finish, which increases the surface hardness enough to use aluminum for things like rear sprockets and belt pulleys.

ABOVE RIGHT: You do not have to have an extravagant paint job on a prize-winning custom; this Battistinis' bike shows class with simple but well-executed paintwork.

BELOW RIGHT: An awful lot of time and money has gone into this amount of chrome-plating!

BELOW: Components such as these risers need to be highly polished before they can be chrome-plated, or machining marks will show right through. If you have access to a spindle polishing machine you can save money by doing this part of the job yourself.

BATTISTINIS

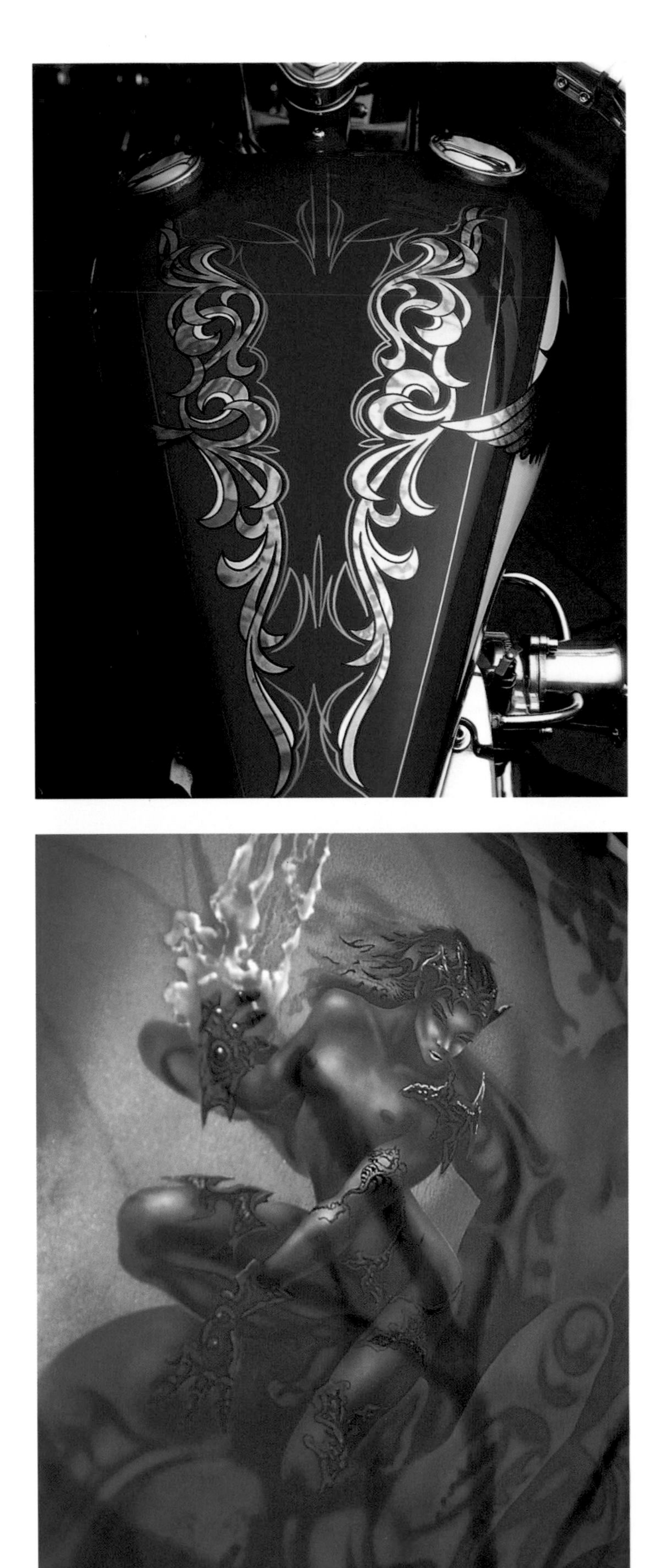

PAINT

The next major type of finishing is paint. As with so many other processes, it starts with cleaning. However this is done, it must be finished off with a solvent that leaves the part absolutely grease-free. Then remember it's important to get a good "key" for paint, otherwise it'll fall off at the first excuse. This is often done using an "acid etch" primer, which chemically keys itself into the surface. Depending on what system of paint you're using, you may have to be really careful that no silicone lubricants have been used nearby. These can ruin a paint job in the minutest of quantities.

Painting is getting more and more specialized as the years go by: the easiest method is spraying — there are many different types of "normal" spray paint, from cellulose to two-pack epoxy. Then there are the more professional stove enamelling and powder coating methods — both of which apply paint and then "cook" it. Some of these paints are very poisonous and require air-fed masks and protective clothing. Local regulations may have forced the spray shops to spend a lot of money on emission control and safety equipment. They'll have to recover this cost somewhere, so if you're getting them to do the work, expect to pay for their experience and investment.

My advice is to find out what's involved in painting by talking to the painters. When you find one that understands what you want, ask to see some examples of his work — if he's any good he'll be proud to show you. Check the finish in good light. The odds are he'll

ABOVE AND ABOVE LEFT: The paint on "Corsa" by Battistinis is a stunning example of this type of work.

LEFT: Some people like murals rather than graphics. This fantasy art scene will have taken a long, long time to produce.

show you any blemishes himself; if he really cares, he'll sound like he's ready to lie on a railway line over some imperfection the rest of us would need an electron microscope to see.

Unfortunately there isn't room in this book to delve into custom painting in detail — there are many different processes, each of which has its own adherents and detractors. All painters have their own methods of working, and some artists are more reliable than others. If you're in any doubt, find some previous customers and talk to them. If they say that the guy took twice as long and cost twice as much as quoted, take heed. Finally, remember you've got to live with the paint scheme you've chosen, so take your time to decide what colors to use and how to style them.

ABOVE RIGHT: The paint on Dave Stewart's trike displays the latest style of wild colors and graphics.

BELOW: A little humor can go a long way . . .

BELOW RIGHT: The paint on this Shovel is stunning, and quite different. Being original is difficult — every time you come up with an idea it seems that someone else has already done it!

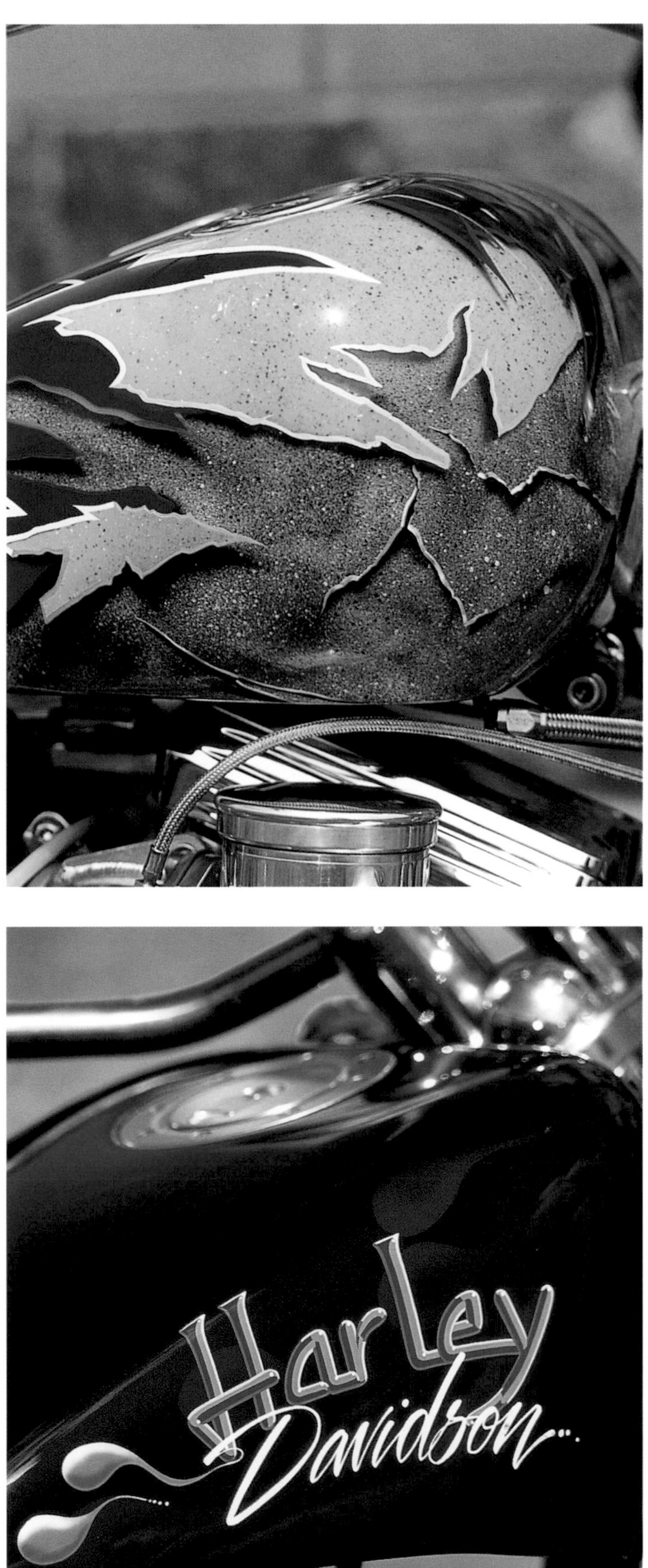

ABOVE LEFT: A spectacular line-up of Ness bikes shows the extremes of paint scheme possible if you have the imagination and the technical skills to reproduce your dreams — if not you'll need the money to pay someone else to burn the midnight oil for you.

BELOW LEFT: Modern paints can be very toxic, and so require heavy investment in equipment. This painter is using an air-fed mask in a proper spray-booth. Pollution regulations require extractors with special filters — all in all, don't expect your paintwork to come cheap! This is Terry Spencer at Battistinis laying a lacquer coat onto the "Dark Angel" frame.

TOP: Native themes are very popular.

TOP LEFT: Flames have always been popular, and will probably never go out of date. They can be mixed with other artwork, as is shown here.

ABOVE LEFT: This Shovel chop shows off another flame-job very well.

ABOVE: This paintwork bears scrutiny up close — there's no telling how many coats of clear laquer it took to achieve this quality of color depth. (See page188 for more of Dave Stewart's trike.

FASTENERS AND PLUMBING

The subject of fasteners basically covers nuts and bolts; in the motorcycle world it's often just called "hardware." It also includes things like rivets and other more specialized methods of joining components without welding. With the exception of those who've worked in the aerospace or motor racing industries, very few custom builders take the trouble to learn anything about hardware, which is a shame. As Carroll Smith states in his excellent series of racing car construction books, "Nothing good has ever been reported about aircraft falling out of the sky." Acquiring a little knowledge about bolt construction is well worth the time and trouble — it could just make you better informed; then again it could save your neck.

If you hear fasteners being described as "high tensile," it usually means they're good quality. Wherever possible use them on your motorcycle. When dealing with threaded fasteners, you'll come across the terms "rolled thread" and "cut thread." This may not appear to be of any particular significance, but it's very important to understand what they mean. A rolled thread is produced by rotating and squeezing the component between two formers. It "cold works" the metal, giving it superior properties, effectively leaving a hard skin to the thread. It also leaves a nice curvature to the base of the thread root.

A cut thread, however, looks the same from a distance. It's produced on a lathe or by hand with a thread die. Get up close and you'll see that the threads appear sharper, which is exactly what they are. If you examined it at a microscopic level, you'd see that the base of the thread was jagged and torn by the machining process. It takes a lot less stress in the thread for it to crack across any of these jagged edges. If this component were somewhere critical — such as in an aircraft — it could cause a lot of people in Carroll Smith's words to "leave the party early."

There are two major categories of threads — metric and non-metric. The aerospace industry is gradually moving over to metric, but in the meantime we have the Unified series — UNF and UNC, which stand for "unified fine" and "unified coarse." Fine threads should only be used either screwed into steel or with a steel nut. Coarse threads, however, are the opposite and should only be used into soft material like aluminum or magnesium. If necessary they can be used with steel nuts in non-critical applications.

There are two major sorts of bolt heads, hex and socket head. Hex head bolts are what we are used to seeing all over the place. They come in a variety of grades and strengths; a 3/8 bolt, for instance, may be good enough to use on the space shuttle or it may be fit only for a shopping trolley. It depends on what alloy of steel was used, its shape, and what heat treatment it has had.

Socket head bolts, often called "Allen bolts," tend to be of a much higher grade than hex heads. Unfortunately, all the really good ones have a poor finish, so they don't look very nice. The exception to this is those made of titanium, but they are so expensive as to be impractical, unless you have access to some via a military surplus yard.

When a bolt fails, there are many possible reasons. The thread may have stripped either from the bolt or from whatever it was screwed into. The bolt may have snapped because of overtightening or overstretching. Then again, it may have sheared because of poor installation, poor component design or overloading. One of the commonest causes of failure is when the bolt simply comes loose and falls out; a more complicated cause is fracture due to stress. This stress usually takes the form of something cyclic, that is something that repeats over and over again — for instance a connecting rod bolt in a car engine. On a Harley the biggest cause of cyclic stress is vibration. This doesn't tend to snap bolts, but it does loosen things unless serious attention is paid to the particular installation.

One of the best ways to stop bolts from coming loose is to lockwire them, a technique taken from the aircraft industry. All you have to do is drill a small hole in one corner of the bolt head and lead a piece of wire to something solid so the bolt can't undo. The wire has to be of the right type, and can be purchased as lockwire (or twistwire) from a variety of sources. It also has to be fitted very carefully: if it's too slack, the bolt will still come loose. If it's too tight, the wire will snap. The correct way is to use special lockwire pliers, which will induce a twist along the wire.

If you're using a bolt with a nut on the end, you can fit a lock-nut. This usually takes the form of a nut with a nylon insert — when you tighten the nut, the insert "grabs" the thread, resulting in a nut that cannot be

RIGHT: Here's a good example of an installation with high grade fasteners — this is a close-up of Graham Duffy's rear wheel, showing the bolt-on spokes. Low-cost hardware is a false economy; a failure may result in damage to the bike and/or personal injury to yourself or others. See the step-by-step section for more about Graham's bike.

TUBELESS
IF FITTED WITH A TUBE
AM23
LOAD RANGE B
MADE IN ENGLAND

shaken loose and yet can be removed with a wrench. Some installations use a second nut — called a check-nut — on the component; its purpose is exactly the same, to stop the item from shaking loose.

If you can't fit lockwire or a lock nut, all is not lost. Use a good solvent to clean both the male and female parts of the thread and then use a drop of thread-locking compound. These chemical locking methods are very good when used in the right manner. The factory uses them extensively but has a lot of knowledge about their workings. There are many different grades, from screw-locking, which gives quite a weak bond, through to engineering adhesives, classed as providing a permanent bond. Because of the color, this sort of permanent bond is sometimes known as "green welding." You can shift these "permanently" bonded parts if you get them hot with a gas torch first. This "kills" the bond very effectively.

FINDING HARDWARE

One of the problems with good hardware is that it can be difficult and/or expensive to get hold of. If you're lucky enough to be near an aircraft dismantlers or surplus house, there's an easy solution to this! Get to know what to look for, and take a micrometer and a magnet along with you. The first is because the military often use slightly oversize bolts, which may or may not be a good thing depending on your installation. The magnet is to check what the material is. If it's magnetic, it'll be steel-based. If not, it could be aluminum, stainless, or titanium. Be very careful using aluminum fasteners, as they're only suitable for certain applications. Stainless is great for most places on a motorcycle but it can be weaker than high tensile steel, so get advice from a professional if in doubt.

If you find some titanium hardware, you're going to need that advice more than ever. It'll be wonderfully light but you need to be very well informed before you use it anywhere important. This is because titanium hardware can be very "notch sensitive," meaning that even a slight scratch can cause a failure. Used properly it can save a lot of weight, hence its popularity in racing bikes.

PLUMBING

We have already seen that custom builders can benefit from the use of aerospace components in many areas — another one of these is plumbing, which on a bike translates into the fuel and oil lines. It's of no surprise that aircraft designers want to make absolutely sure that none of their hydraulic systems fail in use. The advantage for customizers is that we can purchase the same (expensively developed) technology for our bikes.

Basically oil and fuel hoses are just bigger versions of braided brake lines. As mentioned in the section on brakes, Earls, Russell, and Goodridge all supply these fittings. The usual ones are available pre-assembled; however, if you need something made-to-measure, you're going to have to visit a local stockist or get a catalog and do it yourself. If you do the latter, allow enough length to get the hoses out of the way, and have a good think about the problems, such as getting too close to exhausts or suspension parts.

BELOW and RIGHT: Big Al's bike again; there's a serious amount of plumbing going on here! When you're installing fuel lines, they should be high quality. When they're via a fuel pump, you have no choice. Nitrous oxide also requires the best equipment, or someone is going to get hurt. Likewise, oil should be routed through the best lines you can afford. A burst line can result in a trashed motor, and if it gets on your (or someone else's) tires, can result in tragedy.

LEFT: This twin-throat sidedraft Dell Orto carburetor has a braided stainless steel hose supplying the fuel. Note the fitting that connects it to the carb body. Rubber hoses will deteriorate in sunlight and are also susceptible to extremes of temperature — they also don't look nearly as cool as braid.

WHEELS

Wheels come from the manufacturers in two basic formats — spoked and cast. Spoked wheels look nice but they aren't as strong as cast. Cast wheels can run tubeless tires but can't be repaired as easily as spoked ones. And so on. For the custom bike builder there's another choice — billet.

Before the custom builder gets too excited about all the styles available, he needs to decide what sizes the bike is going to require. Harley front wheels are usually of 16, 19, or 21 inches in diameter, and anywhere from 3.00 to 5.10 inches in width. Rear wheels are usually of 16 inches' diameter, and up to 6 inches wide. This is not true for racing, however, where 17 inches is the standard diameter, although there has been some experimentation with 16.5 inches by manufacturers.

For those who like the traditional look of spokes, there's a range of parts available to build wheels with double or triple the usual number of spokes. Stock wheels have 40 spokes, the "extra spoke" custom wheels can have 80, or even 120! If you choose to rebuild your existing wheels and decide to fit new spokes, they can be purchased in either chrome or polished stainless. Chrome spokes look nice but eventually the plating will fall off and rust will set in, whereas stainless ones will look lovely for the life of the bike. Building wheels is a specialist job, so if you haven't done it before, find a wheel builder to do it for you unless you feel like a challenge.

If you do feel confident enough to try it yourself, take your time and use an anti-seize compound on the spoke threads. Make sure the rim isn't dented or buckled, or you'll never get it true. The best way to go about building a wheel is either to make a detailed drawing before you strip it, or to borrow another wheel so you can copy the spoke layout as you lace it.

My technique when truing up is to mount the wheel in an old swing arm and spin it, holding a large marker pen close to the spinning rim. Where the pen marks, there's a high spot — so I then pull the opposite spokes up a little. Doing this a little at a time will get the wheel true — but remember to get all the spokes to the same tension, and never overtighten them or they'll snap.

RIGHT: Most traditional wheels have 40 spokes, but they can be built with 80 or even 120. This '97 FXR, built by Big Jack's Cycle, has an 80-spoke wheel fitted.

BELOW RIGHT: This Ness Shovel/Knuck has traditional 40-spoke wheels. Simple and clean, they still have their place in customizing.

BELOW: This wheel on Graham Duffy's AMS bike is at the opposite extreme from those opposite. It's CNC-machined from billet alloy, and features an inboard disc with CNC sprocket and caliper carrier. This picture was taken part-way through its construction, before final polishing.

BELOW LEFT: Detail of the fasteners on the same wheel seen from the other side.

Oxygen
METZELER

ABOVE: Solid disc wheels have their adherents, but steering can suffer in high side winds.

BELOW: Disc side of Performance Machine "Aero" wheel from Battistinis "Coupé De Ville," featured later in this book.

The correct tool to adjust spokes is a purpose-made "key"; however, after years of building wheels I've settled on using a very small adjustable wrench. Used spoke nipples are often damaged by previous mechanics — so I find I can adjust the wrench to fit each individual nipple which minimizes further damage. If I'm going to work on a used wheel, I soak the nipples in a fluid such as WD40 several hours beforehand. This allows time for it to penetrate along the threads, so they're freed off when I come to work on it.

There are times when the spokes have been so badly corroded that no amount of persuasion will undo the nipples. When this is the case I reach for the disc cutter. Great care must be taken to avoid damaging the rim or hub when removing spokes like this, and — as usual — eye protection is a must.

Custom wheels are available in a variety of styles and materials. They can be purchased constructed from cast or billet aluminum. For racing-only purposes there are many magnesium wheels on the market but they're very expensive and don't last very long. These are the lightest of all the options open — with the

possible exception of carbon fiber, which, once built into a wheel, is about the same weight.

Probably the single most important thing to a custom builder concerning wheels is how they look. They come in every conceivable design from solid disc to wild swirls. Performance Machine supplies custom wheels and brakes, as does Arlen Ness. Both have been in the business for years, during which time they have built up excellent reputations.

While we're on the subject of wheels, don't forget to get some decent tires — it's never worth spending countless amounts of money on the rest of the bike, and then throwing it down the road because the tires weren't up to the job.

RIGHT: Three-spoke CNC wheels look good on the right bike. This one is on the front of "Warbird," by Battistinis.

BELOW: Another close-up of Performance Machine's "Aero" wheel.

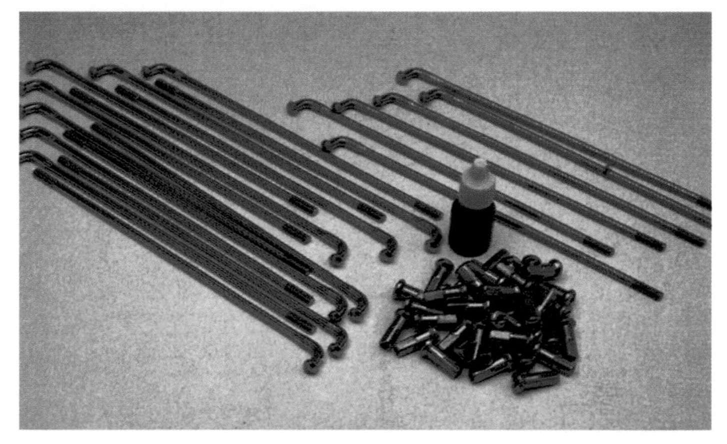

ABOVE: Performance Machine "Flamed" style billet wheel.

ABOVE RIGHT: Arlen Ness billet spoke wheel hubs . . .

RIGHT: . . . And the stainless steel spoke set.

FAR RIGHT: Riding like this will wear your tires out in no time. This is ex-GP racer Paul Lewis.

BELOW: Chromed Ness-Tech spoke wheels, using chromed hubs and rims, with stainless steel spokes.

Harley
Davidson

SUSPENSION

Suspension can be subdivided into two main areas — front and rear. While all modern bikes have some form of suspension at the front, this is not entirely true of the rear. Some people still build and ride rigids, which we'll examine in detail a little later on.

FRONT SUSPENSION

There are various possible routes when considering what to do with the front end. First, you have got to decide on the length of the forks — you can fit a long set, a short set, or leave them the same length. This is pretty much dictated by the style you've chosen. For instance, if you've chosen to build a lowrider, you're not going to want to fit a set of long front forks.

Once the length has been decided, the next step is to choose what type of forks you want. If you're after the Retro 1950s' look, then maybe a set of Heritage-style springers will suit you. However, if you're a performance nut, then you might be turned on by the look of a set of upside-down forks, as used on the factory VR1000 race bike. Alternatively you may like the look of the stock forks but just want them to be a different length. One way to achieve this is to purchase a pair of aftermarket fork tubes, which means that you can extend or shorten them. In the latter case it's easier to purchase a fork lowering kit that contains shorter springs and new spacers.

For years it was fashionable to mount the lower legs up in a lathe and machine them down for a cleaner look. These were then appropriately known as "turned legs." These days you can purchase chromed billet aluminum legs with all manner of decorative machining, hidden axle mountings, and so on. Likewise there are also high quality centerless ground fork tubes to match the legs.

Once you've got your fork requirements worked out, there are still many other things that can be done to fine-tune them to your needs. For instance, chang-

BELOW: Graham Duffy's AMS bike front end; these are Italian "upside-down," or "inverted" forks made by Ceriani.

LEFT: Seen prior to the dry build . . .

RIGHT: . . . and installed on the finished bike.

ing the volume of oil in the forks, and altering the oil's viscosity with a different SAE grade can make big improvements. You can also purchase spring kits made by people like Progressive Suspension or White Bros.; these feature improved spring rates that can significantly improve a bike's handling.

ABOVE LEFT: Telescopic forks shown with springs removed — hence they are in the fully compressed position. These are 41mm FLH units, heavily polished.

ABOVE: Modern Evolution engined bike with old-style Springer forks.

REAR SUSPENSION

Not all bikes, especially custom Harley-Davidsons, have rear suspension. The ones that don't are usually referred to as "rigids" and are also appropriately known as a "hardtails." A concession to the rider is sometimes made in the form of a sprung seat, although this is by no means always the case. Rigids can lead to back trouble and kidney problems if prolonged journeys are made on rough roads.

The modern answer is to make the bike look like a rigid, while still having suspension movement — the Harley factory achieved this with the Softail frame. They did it by making a swing arm that looked like the back of a rigid frame but which had two shock absorbers hidden away under the transmission. People want their bike to look like a rigid because the lines are very clean and uncluttered, so this is a classic example of engineering a bike for looks rather than function.

It's possible to implement rear suspension that looks like a rigid by other methods, such as with a monoshock. This is where the swing arm is again made to look like a Hardtail rear end, but instead of mounting two shocks under the bike, a single unit is fitted under the seat. The problem with this method is that it limits the components that can be fitted in this area of the bike, such as the battery and rear exhaust pipe.

TOP: Plunger suspension shown during a dry-build. Note the TIG welds visible on the frame. Many people, myself included, think it's a shame to mold over good quality welding.

ABOVE: Good old Harley-style telescopic rear shocks are still popular.

RIGHT: Early Harleys had no rear suspension at all; rigid bikes live on to this day in many traditional chops

However, for the performance enthusiast it means that a racing damper unit can be fitted, with a commensurate leap in suspension control. For someone seriously interested in blowing away the opposition, this has to be the way to go.

One of the added advantages of using a monoshock damper unit from a racing bike is that it's possible to engineer an adjustable linkage between the swinging arm and the damper. This means that the ratio of wheel to damper movement can be tuned to suit the individual rider's preferences.

ABOVE RIGHT: Grand Prix rear monoshock damper fitted to my racer. Note fully adjustable linkage to vary lever ratio.

CENTER RIGHT: Another "plunger" set-up, this time on "Corsa," a Sportster built by Battistinis.

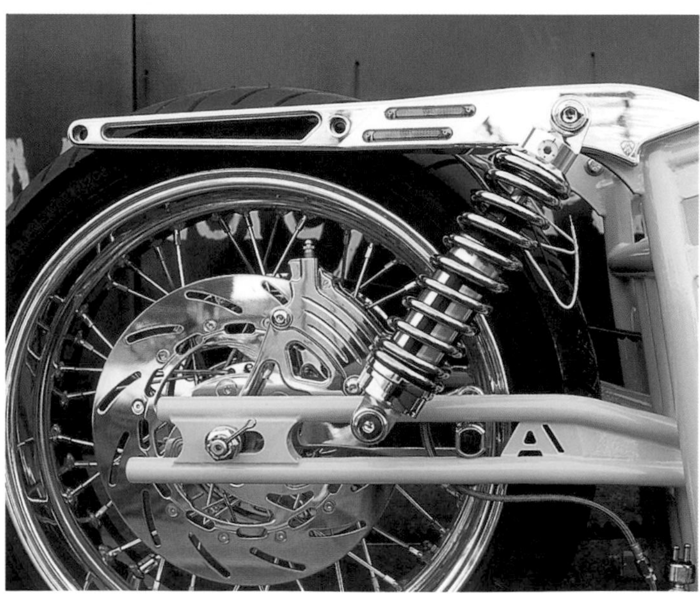

BELOW RIGHT: Traditional coil-over-damper Progressive Suspension shocks, fitted to an Arlen Ness rolling chassis.

BELOW: Another monoshock damper system, this time on "Sandstorm," by Battistinis during a dry-build.

BRAKES

When you're working out how you're going to configure your front end, you need to take into account what sort of brakes you want. These days it's cool to have serious brakes. In the old days it was *de rigeur* to have no front brake at all, which was fine if there were no cars or unexpected corners around. For years the choice was restricted to drum brakes — a system where two "friction shoes" were applied to the inside of the wheel hub by a hand-operated lever and cable. These were generally fairly weak by modern standards but, with the advent of hydraulic discs, some powerful brakes became available.

For years fitting a set of aftermarket calipers made a big difference over the stock ones — but at last the factory is producing bikes with some reasonable braking power. Companies like Performance Machine can supply you with many different braking set-ups. The choice of brakes is basically centered around how many pistons the caliper has — generally the more pistons, the stronger the brake will be.

Early calipers had either one piston, and a sliding body, or two opposed pistons. It was also usual to have a single disc at the front but, as riders demanded better braking, twin discs became optional and, later, often standard. Newer designs for more powerful brakes had four pistons per caliper and, later still, six. I wonder how long it will be before eight-piston calipers become the norm?

Most road bikes have a single two-piston caliper on the rear, but it has become fashionable to fit some really outrageous brakes to the rear of custom Harleys. Take a look at the photos to see some bikes with two calipers or even two four-piston calipers mounted onto the same disc! It is not unknown for some

BELOW: Performance Machine four-piston calipers fitted to twin drilled discs on an Arlen Ness bike.

RIGHT: Arlen Ness bike fitted with six-piston calipers on large floating drilled discs.

BELOW RIGHT: AP Racing Grand Prix four-piston calipers fitted to 320mm floating discs, on my racer. When necessary I have twin carbon fiber discs which can be swapped at short notice.

FAR RIGHT: Way over the top! Four six-piston calipers fitted to twin discs. This guy really wanted some stopping power!

BILLET-6
BILLET-6
BILLET-6

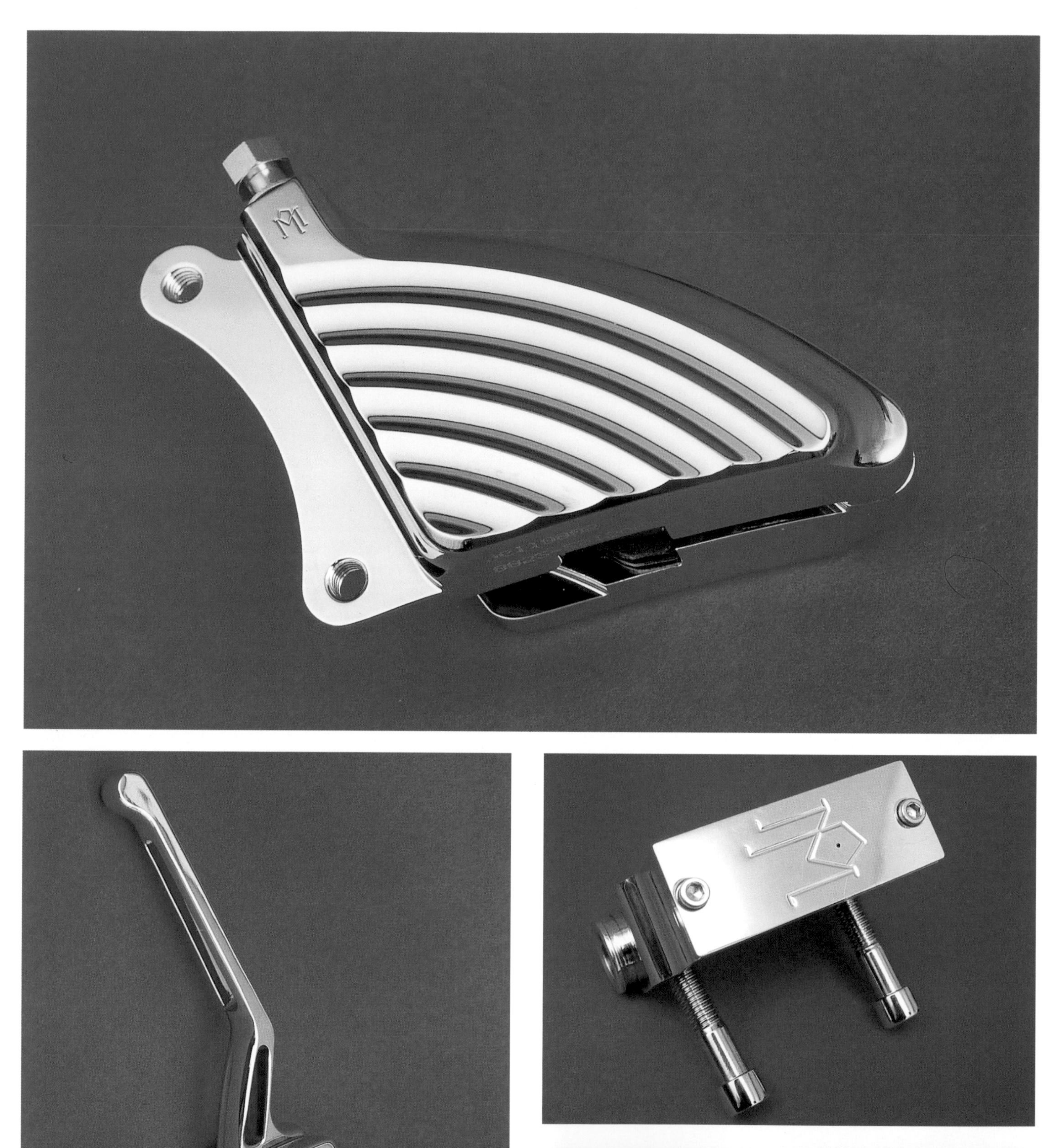

5/8

LEFT: Performance Machine CNC billiet caliper.

BELOW LEFT: Performance Machine rear master cylinder.

BOTTOM LEFT: Just below the temporary dust seal on this Performance Machine rear master cylinder, you can see the piston size marked, in this case it is 5/8. This information can be useful when matching components.

FAR LEFT: Ness-Tech "Radius" CNC billet front brake master cylinder.

custom builders to turn the rear sprocket into a brake disc for the cleanest look possible. The downside to this is that it gets really expensive every time the sprocket needs replacing.

One of the best possible investments you can make is to fit some braided stainless steel brake hoses to your motorcycle. The stock rubber ones deteriorate over the years, especially when exposed to ultra-violet from sunlight. Even when new, the rubber hoses will swell under the pressure produced by braking — this lessens the amount of feel the rider has, and the amount of power available at the disc. A set of steel lines will last for years and will not swell under braking pressures. This will give the rider that extra power and control when he needs it most.

Braided steel hoses are available from a variety of suppliers, including Earls, Russell, and Goodridge. They are supplied to length, and can have end fittings of different types and materials. When you're ordering your hoses, make sure that you've allowed for full suspension travel and any changes in fork length you're going to make. Also check the hose entry points on the calipers if you are changing them as well.

It's worth taking the time to make sure the fittings you're supplied with fit properly — there are several different hose angles for each type. Another thing to get right is the choice of metal from which the fitting is constructed; you can purchase cadmium-plated steel, anodized aluminum, stainless steel, and titanium.

Aluminum and titanium hose ends are intended for racing and are not really suitable for road use (besides, they can be very expensive), so the usual choice is down to cad-plate or stainless. My opinion is that it's worth the extra money for stainless, which will outlast the bike and still look good, whereas cad-plate will go dull and corrode at the first sign of winter.

If you're going to leave the stock brakes in place, it's worth stripping and cleaning them. Examine everything — the hoses in particular — to check for malfunction or damage: in particular, check that the caliper pistons move in and out freely. If the pistons are sticking, your bike is potentially lethal — so remove, clean, and replace them. If you have not performed this task before, do so very carefully — or take them to a trustworthy repair shop. If the rubber seals get damaged or the piston bores get scored, the brake will not work properly.

When you reassemble the brakes, take the trouble to grease the bleed screw with an anti-seize compound. This will help you next time you work on the brakes — it's a pain in the neck (and the wallet) if the screw rounds off or snaps, requiring a trip to a machine shop to get it sorted out. You'll also need to replace the fluid and bleed the air out. Make sure that you're using the right grade of fluid — if there is any doubt refer to the factory manuals for your model. Then make sure that the area you're working in is clean and dust-free or you'll end up with dirt in the fluid, which is a sure-fire route to brake trouble.

If you experience trouble getting all of the air out of the system, try removing the caliper from the bike and putting a piece of metal between the pads — a flat tire-iron usually works well. Then hold the caliper at different angles while you bleed it to dislodge any air bubbles trapped in the system — sometimes tapping the hose with a wrench helps here. When you've bled the system fully, take the time to make sure the hoses are clear of any moving parts. Bear in mind also that braided hoses will wear through chrome or alloy very quickly if allowed to do so. There are many ways to secure them out of harm's way, from zip ties to custom billet hose clamps.

Another way to increase braking performance is to fit some good quality brake pads, such as Ferodo, EBC, or SBS. These are a marked improvement over the stock items, though they may well not last as long; nevertheless the extra power (and safety) is a good investment.

So far no mention has been made of the handlebar master cylinder, which is where all the hydraulic pressure is generated. If you fit some high-performance calipers, you're going to have to fit a matching master cylinder — the stock one will not be up to the job and could even result in weaker brakes than before! Likewise, if you upgrade from single to twin discs, you'll need to fit a twin-disc model master cylinder.

There are some really nice products in the marketplace these days, but do take informed advice from professionals to find out which master cylinders will work with which calipers. Much the same can be said for the rear master cylinder — if you fit multi-calipers, or just a multi-piston caliper, you'll need to check their compatibility.

There are many rear master cylinders available, from copies of the original equipment, through to

Harley Davidson
Electra Glide
TOKICO

CNC-machined aircraft-grade aluminum billet examples. They can be purchased chromed or highly polished — as discussed in the section on finishing, it's down to you as the builder to choose which you want.

It's very important to ensure that modifications made to the brakes are engineered correctly. It's no good constructing a footpeg linkage that looks great if it's going to lock-up the first time you use it in anger — especially as this will probably be the first time a truck pulls out in front of you. As I said earlier, even if you decide you don't need to upgrade your brakes yet, it's well worth overhauling your current set-up. Strip the whole system down, clean everything with an approved brake solvent, and check all the components are within recommended tolerances. There's no excuse not to these days, as all the parts you could possibly need are available in various rebuild kits — this certainly wasn't the case until recent years.

Don't forget whenever you go near brake fluid that it'll seriously damage paintwork in seconds — so if you spill some on your gastank or whatever, wash the spillage off with water immediately. My favored choice is to remove the brakes from the bike as a whole system. I then work on them well away from the bike, as brake fluid has a habit of splashing unnoticed until the next morning when it's too late.

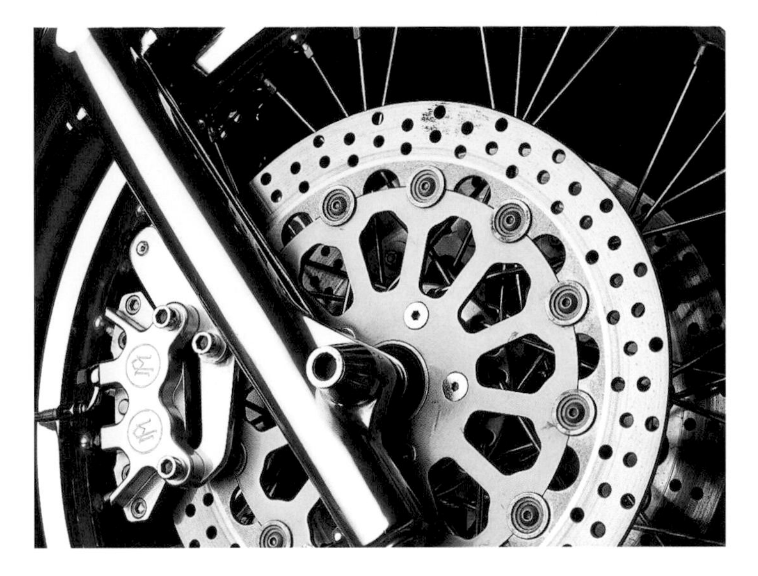

ABOVE: A Battistinis bike with twin four-piston Performance Machine calipers on massive floating discs with lightweight central carriers.

ABOVE LEFT: Although dressers are not performance machines, due to their weight they often benefit from from brake upgrades.

BELOW LEFT: Twin four-piston Tokico calipers and discs salvaged from a Japanese sports bike. This can be a cost effective way of getting hold of high power brakes.

FAR LEFT: JayBrake four-piston front caliper from Arlen Ness.

BELOW: Single-piston Swedish ISR one-piece caliper. This is a nicely made unit, but I doubt it will stop a Harley very well.

ELECTRICS

The single most ignored area when custom bikes are built is the electrical system. At one time I earned a living wiring up people's customs — mostly there had been no thought given whatsoever as to how the electrics were going to be installed. Often the electrics box was purchased and fitted without any regard as to what had to fit inside.

Very few custom builders give any thought to using the right gauge wire, and it's very common for people make a wiring harness to use wires that are all the same color. It'll work just fine, but when there's a fault it's very difficult to identify exactly which wire is which.

If you want to do the electrics yourself, take your time. A good way to do it is to buy a wiring loom from a wrecking yard; from this you can build a rough but functional test harness for your bike. When you've done this, and satisfied yourself that everything works, you can modify it to fit perfectly (not forgetting to test with the handlebars turned from lock to lock). Then you can construct one using good quality wire, confident you've got a tidy installation.

Something that separates the amateur from the professional is the way the harness is finished off. The commonest way is to spiral wrap it with electrical tape, but the best way is to use heatshrink tubing. This has a plastic sheath which fits loosely over the wires; when warmed with a heat gun, the tubing shrinks to a tight fit. It takes familiarity to get a really tidy installation, but it's well worth the extra time and expense.

A common fault with Harley electrics is caused by the plug from the alternator to the rectifier/regulator box working loose. This can cause all sorts of problems, not the least of which is a flat battery. If you have to replace any of the electrical components, particularly the rectifier/regulator box, it's well worth considering purchasing one with a lifetime guarantee.

Something else that's worth remembering is that if you leave the battery unattended for a long time without charging it, you run the risk of ruining it. This is easily forgotten over the months it can take to build a good custom, and by the time you need the battery to start the bike, it's too late.

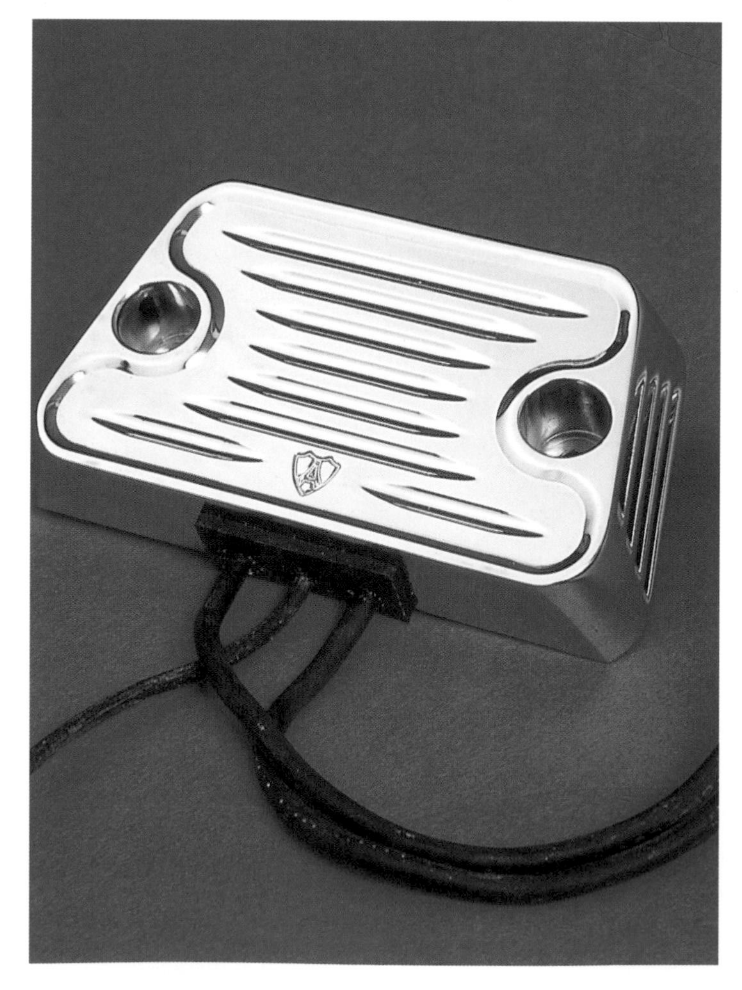

ABOVE: "Billet Wedge" voltage regulator from Ness-Tech.

RIGHT: Classic style tail light on "Matt's Pan."

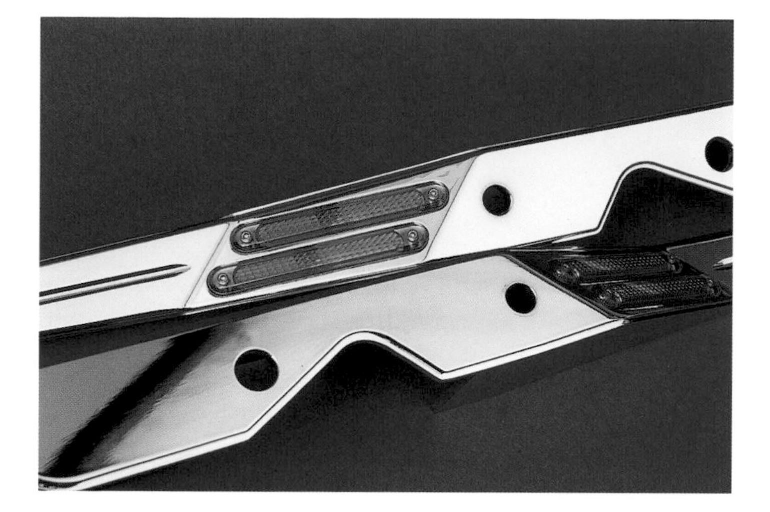

TOP: FXR fender struts from Ness-Tech with integral turn signal lights.

ABOVE RIGHT: Correct battery installation is vital — if the vent gets blocked the battery will split, and dump acid all over your bike. If the terminals pull off, your bike will stop, and if they short out it will catch fire!

RIGHT: High performance starters help to spin over big-inch motors.

BELOW RIGHT: This bike is mid-way through being wired in the Battistinis' workshops.

If you have to fit any switches on the bike, two good sources are marine and aerospace supply houses. The two main enemies of all electrical systems are damp and vibration. If you have electrical problems look for a sort of green "fur" around any terminals or contacts. This is caused by a chemical reaction which separates copper out of the brass parts of the terminals, which turns green in color. A good place not to buy switches for use on motorcycles is from automotive shops, which don't generally understand (or care) about the demands we make of our bikes.

Another thing to avoid from the automotive market is the crimp-on connector, often seen with a blue or red plastic cover. Whenever I'm called in to find a fault on a motorcycle's electrics, the first thing I do is look to see if it has any of these fitted. If there are, nine times out of ten when I get rid of them, the fault disappears. If you must use them, cut the plastic cover off, and solder them in place.

Whenever I used to build a custom harnesses, I always offered the customer the choice of a "normal" or a "one-piece" loom. By one-piece I mean that basically there are no connectors. It does mean that if any major components are removed you don't have the luxury of unplugging them for easy service. However, it's no big deal to cut the wires and re-solder them. The bonus is that electrical harness failures were almost unknown — I never had one brought back to be fixed.

LIGHTS

When you come to purchase lights, you're going to have to weigh the issues of sleek looks against a good light beam. If you never ride at night, or only ride in well-lit city streets, then you don't need to think too hard about it. However, if you live outside the city limits and ride a lot at night, give the light output top priority. There are some very good quartz halogen lights on the market but you need to know a few things about these if you decide to use them. Halogen bulbs are much brighter than the old pre-focus bulbs or the sealed beam units with which we're all familiar. However, they need a stable voltage or else their life is reduced dramatically — so if you run a magneto and no battery, forget halogen bulbs.

Another thing to remember is that if you have to fit a new bulb, never touch the "glass" part of the bulb. This is what the manufacturers refer to as a "quartz envelope" — a special kind of glass able to withstand very high temperatures but very sensitive to the acids in human sweat. The small amount of acid on our hands is enough to cause premature failure.

The bottom line with electrics is that cheap parts and laziness will leave you at the roadside, whereas good parts and a thorough attention to detail will get you there.

ABOVE: Some people like lots of lights!

BELOW AND RIGHT: Others prefer one high-power halogen unit.

H4
MOTORCYCLE
MADE IN JAPAN
SAE M79

RIGHT: Lights on a bike; lights on a truck.

LEFT: This tail light installation and paintwork combine to show a sense of humor.

BELOW: Ness-Tech "Radial" CNC billet tailllight with light bar mounted below.

BOTTOM: Graham Duffy's AMS bike taillight CNC machined from billet aluminum — a very sleek design.

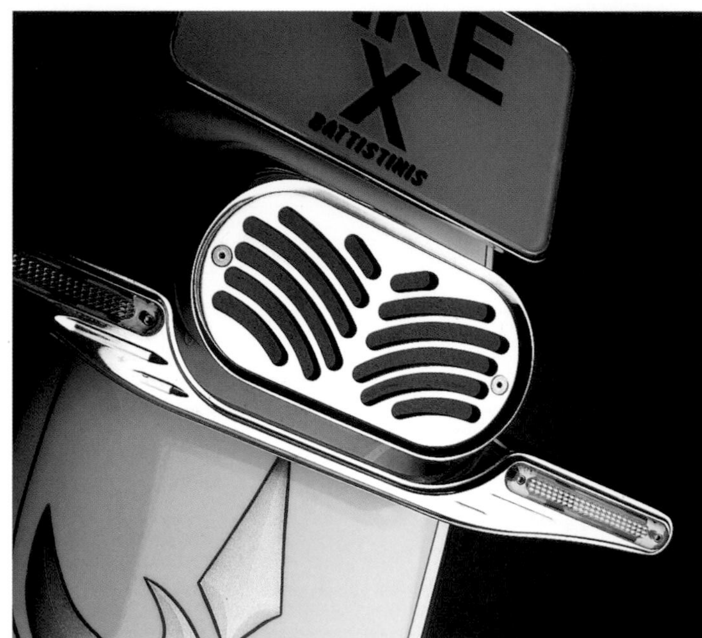

KW
HARLEY DAVIDSON
WORTH

GAS TANK

When it comes to choosing a gas tank, you probably don't need to think too hard; most riders already know what they want. It's got to be a "king sportster," maybe a "fat bob," or then again a "mustang." Whether it's one of these, or something else, gas tank choice is really personal. To some extent the type of riding you do will influence what you need — a long distance cruiser wants all the gas capacity it can get, and then some.

One of the most overlooked parts of the gas tank is the tap. Most taps are incapable of passing enough fuel even for a stocker, let alone a modified bike. If you have a big-inch motor, you're going to need the best fuel supply you can get. You can purchase high-flow taps from Pingel in a variety of types and flow rates. If you want something a bit different, check out the aircraft component suppliers' catalogs. If you're fortunate enough to live near an aircraft dismantling yard, check it out. The cost of new aerospace parts is prohibitive, whereas used parts are almost given away. I really enjoy sorting through these surplus supply houses — they're Aladdin's caves of good things. While we're on this subject, aircraft fuel filler caps are an excellent addition to any modern bike. They mount flush, so if nothing else, they're inherently safer in the event of a crash, but they also look really trick. These days I always fit them whenever possible. You do need to think hard about the angle the tank is going to sit at before you decide where to fit the filler cap. You could end up not being able to fill it more than, say, two thirds if you're not careful — trust me, it's easily done.

FENDERS

The lines of the tank, seat, and handlebars will more or less dictate what type of fenders you're going to fit. They're available in steel, fiberglass, ABS plastic, and

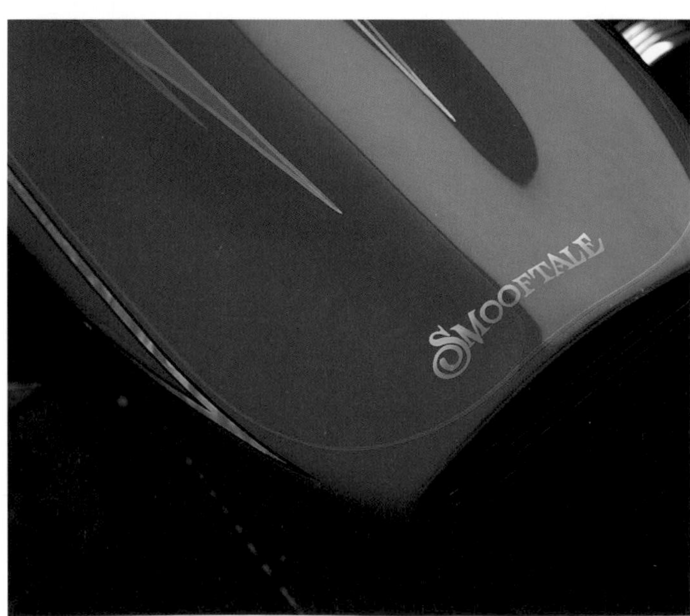

TOP LEFT: The extended air scoop on this Ness bike gives it a dragster look.

CENTER LEFT AND ABOVE RIGHT: Gas tank size is often dictated by the type of riding you do. Long distance bikes need lots of fuel capacity.

LEFT: Shaped rear fender on "Smooftale," by Battistinis.

RIGHT: Flush mount filler caps are a really good idea. Not only do they look good and work well, but in the event of a collision, you'll do yourself less damage than by sliding over the cap in the picture above.

aluminum, in many different widths and depths. You can purchase them with ducktail ends, others for springers, dressers, fatbobs, and so on. It pays to make sure that the mounting brackets are solid and secure — it's not uncommon for fender-mounting hardware to foul the rear tire and cause severe damage to it. Don't forget that, unless you're running a rigid, you're going to have to allow for suspension movement.

FOOTPEG ASSEMBLIES

We haven't covered footpeg assemblies in any detail yet. In the section on carburetors we mentioned that the air cleaner can foul your leg, so remember this point when choosing your assembly. One of the most important things to get right when building a bike is the relationship between the footpegs and the handle-

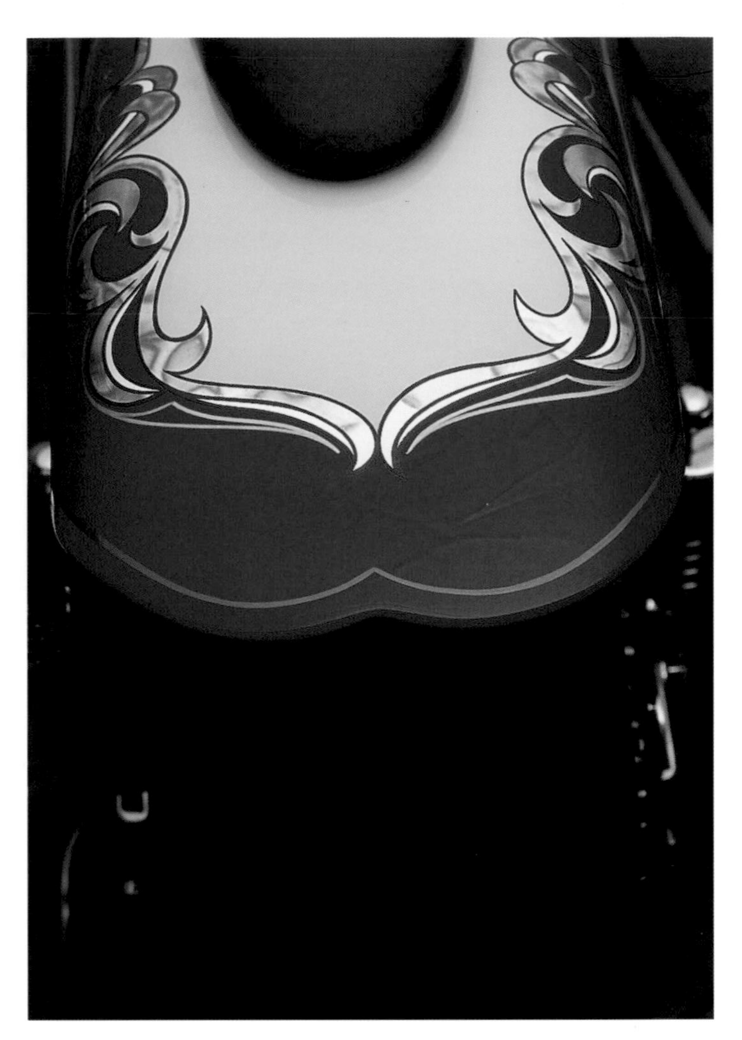

RIGHT AND FAR RIGHT: Shaping the rear fender is not hard to do, but adds that extra style if it is matched to the theme of the bike. This is "Corsa" by Battistinis.

BELOW: Oil tank installation, again on "Corsa."

BELOW RIGHT AND BOTTOM RIGHT: Wild fenders from who else, but Arlen Ness.

ME1
ARLEN NESS

bars. If the relationship is not correct, you won't feel right, and furthermore you won't look right.

Some riders will only mount forward controls on their bikes; others only fit rear mounts — it's down to your preferred style of riding. If you like blasting through canyons, then you'd better think about getting those pegs towards the back. Conversely, if you like to kick back and cruise, get 'em up front.

SEATS

Once you've chosen your gas tank, it's time to sort out what kind of seat you need. Again, it's more important to figure out what kind of use the bike is going to get before you choose something that looks good, but is in reality quite inappropriate. There's a wide range of beautiful seats produced these days by the likes of Mike Corbin and Danny Gray, so there's no excuse (except maybe a lack of cash) to fit something that doesn't match the overall style of the bike and its use.

HANDLEBARS

There are few things that influence the overall look of a bike as much as the handlebars. You can completely ruin the lines of a bike with a poor choice, so it's worth

LEFT: Billet forward controls seen on beautifully built Evolution Big Twin . . .

BELOW: . . . and on this stunning French-built custom.

ABOVE RIGHT: A close-up of Graham Duffy's bike's CNC billet forward controls.

RIGHT: The shifter rod here is of a slotted pattern.

BELOW RIGHT: A different style again — this one has a diamond-pattern rod.

FAR RIGHT: Seats vary from deep and plush on a long-distance tourer, to a piece of aluminum sheet on a dragster. This bike's seat is a custom-made leather item in two colors.

kicking back and thinking this part over. Fortunately, if you do make a mistake, it's not difficult to rectify, in terms of either cost or trouble. If you're unsure what will look right, try to find a dealer who will let you bolt various sets on your bike. If you're going to do this, take some tape with you to wrap them with — the dealer won't thank you if you damage the chrome.

Some of the names given to the various handlebar styles can be pretty obvious — such as "flats" or "T-bars." However, some are rather obscure, names like

"highway," "dresser," and "buckhorn" don't give much of a clue to shape. It's a good idea, therefore, to find a parts' catalog which shows all the different types available. Don't forget that Harleys have one-inch diameter bars, whereas almost every other motorcycle uses ⅞ths of an inch. This is particularly easy to forget when you're purchasing parts like front brake master cylinders.

The most important thing of all is to make sure the bars fit you properly and that the bike is safe to ride for its intended purpose: it's no good fitting 16-inch bars on a long-distance tourer. When you've decided on what you want, there are still a few things to watch out for. If you're using low bars of some description, make sure they'll clear the gas tank at full lock. There's very little to compare with the frustration of chipping your brand new paint job by forgetting to check this first.

If you're altering their height, you'll need to change the length of the control cables. Purchase the very best quality cables that you can find. If you've ever experienced cable failure you'll know that this is good advice. If you're lucky, it happens near your home or a parts store. If not, you could be in the middle of nowhere or, worse still, lying injured in the road somewhere.

You've also got to decide whether you want your bars to be finished with chrome or made of stainless steel. You can also get aircraft aluminum bars but these are more for racing. As usual, my favored choice is to go for the long lasting qualities of stainless.

It's possible to purchase handlebar controls that allow the builder to route the cables inside the bars. This can clean up the looks of the front of the bike enormously: be aware though that, if you're after practicality first and foremost, these bars can be a pain in the neck in the event of a breakage — they can be extremely difficult to get in place at the side of a road.

There is another way to set the bars to the height of your choice, and that's to fit custom risers. The riser is the clamp that bolts the bars to the triple tree, and custom ones can be purchased in a variety of heights or can be made to your own specification. There are many styles, shapes and material choices here: whatever you choose, make sure all mounting hardware is good quality.

While you're checking out the shelves of billet parts on sale, you may like to examine the handlebar controls in this part of the store. Before you go parting with your hard-earned cash, have a think about whether you could live with solid grips. The rubber ones you probably already have might not look as good, but they do filter out quite a lot of vibration. If you're only intending to go boulevard cruising then it's not such a problem, but if you're planning to run coast-to-coast, think again.

CONTROLS AND CLOCKS

If you purchase (or make) some controls — wherever they're mounted — make sure the operating mechanisms work properly. If there's some form of linkage — a personal hate of mine I have to confess — make sure any clevis or heim joints fitted are good quality. One of the easiest ways to ruin a bike is to fit low grade joints to the gearshift linkages. Fit the best you can afford, for cheap ones will not only make the gearshift sloppy, but if one breaks it can be a pain in the neck to fix.

Sooner or later you're likely to consider changing the clocks. Some people, including myself, like to have a minimum of instrumentation — less to go wrong, less weight and less expense. On a long haul, though, it's nice to know your oil pressure is up and your alternator's still charging. All the old traditional styles are still available, from the large "in your face" types, through to the mini "hide 'em away" ones. These days though, you've also got the choice of purchasing digi-

RIGHT: Drag bars are ever-popular; these are the Ness variation on the theme.

BELOW RIGHT: Shortened Beach bars for "Coupé De Ville" by Battistinis.

BELOW: Ness-Tech CNC billet "Diamond Twister" handlebar grips allow the builder to continue his chosen theme still further on the bike.

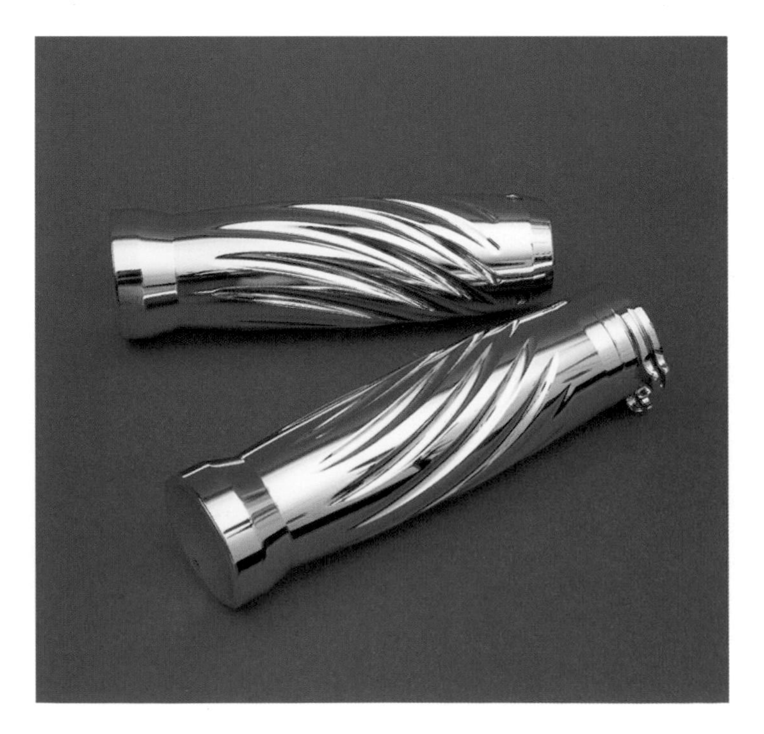

Quality Mo
rcycle Parts

tal electronic displays. One of the advantages of these is that you can dispense with speedo and tach drive cables. A thin (easily hidden away) signal wire is all that's needed. An electronic sender unit called a transducer replaces the speedometer drive unit. You've got to decide for yourself whether this'll suit your ride.

TOP: The electronic readout is mounted in the center of the gas tank on Dave Stewart's trike.

ABOVE: An oil pressure gauge is a good investment, and can also look trick — see the Ness unit earlier in the book.

TOP RIGHT AND OPPOSITE PAGE, TOP LEFT: Instruments and switches mounted in the central dash are very traditional and popular . . .

RIGHT: . . . as they are in the headlight.

TOP RIGHT: Handlebar-mounted mini-instruments are simple and work well.

ABOVE: Ness-Tech billet "Cateye" mirror and turn signal.

RIGHT: Hand shift lever. You won't find this one in the factory parts list!

STEP-BY-STEP GUIDES

PAINT IT BLACK

This bike is one of several meticulously built by Battistinis, in Poole, England. These bikes were built to showcase their workmanship and the parts they sell. Battistinis are the European distributors for Arlen Ness and Performance Machine. They also manufacture and distribute their own products. This bike, "Paint It Black," was built as an update of a bike that Rikki and Dean Battistini built several years ago, which had won them worldwide acclaim. The new version was intended to be the lowrider supreme, using the latest Ness engine covers on a Patrick Racing billet engine. The lines were to be clean and long; judge the result for yourself.

1 2 Here are right- and left-hand views of the frame and swing arm from which it's all to start. It's a 1997 Softail that has been stretched five inches, and had the steering head kicked out to 35° by Battistinis' own Rick James.

Owner	Battistinis
Model	Softail
Builder	Rikki Battistini
Build time	6 months
Engine	1997 Evo, 1,450cc (88cu. in.)
Cases	S & S
Heads	Patrick Racing Billet
Cylinders	Patrick Racing Billet
Ignition	Crane Hi4 Electronic
Carburetor	S & S Super E
Engine covers and accessories	Arlen Ness
Exhausts	Arlen Ness
Transmission	1997 5-Speed (polished)
Primary drive	Chain
Final drive	O ring chain
Paintwork	Jeff McCann Custom Paintwork
Molding	Kirk Jennin, California
Frame	1997, Rick James modified, 5-inch stretch, 35° rake
Shocks	Progressive, chromed
Forks	Battistinis custom
Triple trees	Ness billet narrow glide
Wheels	Chromed Akront rims, Ness hubs
Tires	Metzeler 80/90 x 21 inch and 180/55 x 18 inch
Brakes	Ness calipers on Ness "Smooth 7" rotors
Handlebars	Battistinis custom
Grips and Footpegs	Ness
Fenders	Battistinis custom aluminum
Headlight	Ness
Gas and Oil tanks	Battistinis custom aluminum
Electrics	Battistinis Switchlogic

3 And here's the carburetor, air cleaner, and manifold. It's a good idea to fit them all together before they are installed so that you can check things like bolt thread lengths, hose entry angles, and mounting bracket clearances.

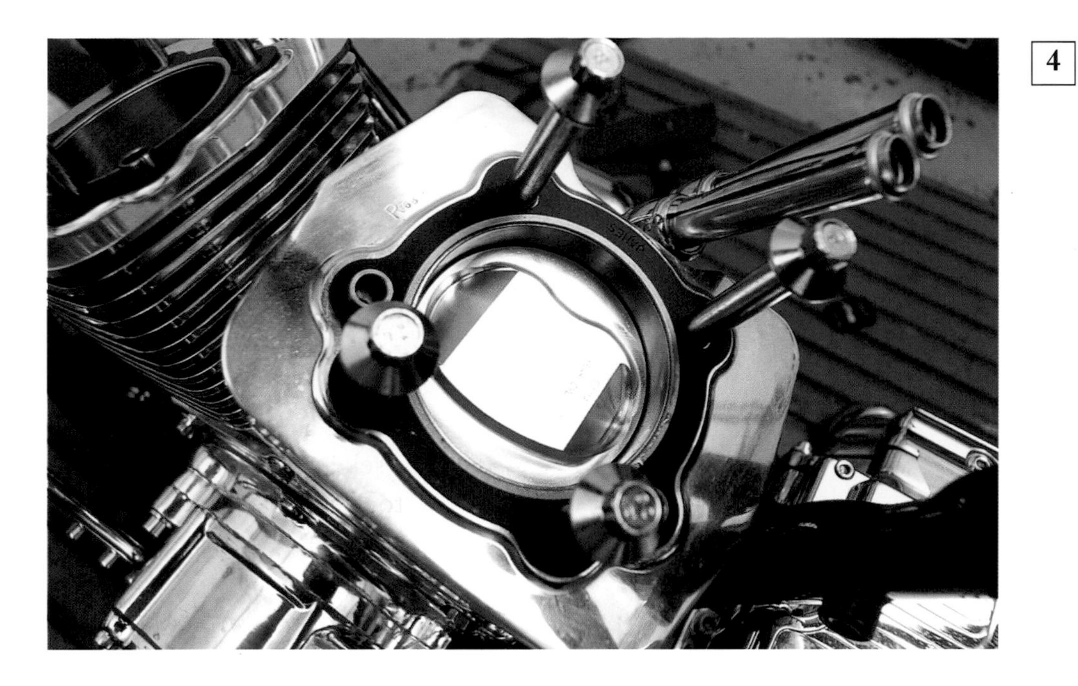

4 Here the bottom end of the motor is installed. The cases are S&S, onto which Patrick Racing billet cylinders have been added.

5 Now the Patrick Racing billet cylinder heads have been fitted, and the installation of the rear fender and seat is being checked . . .

6 The same from the right-hand side . . .

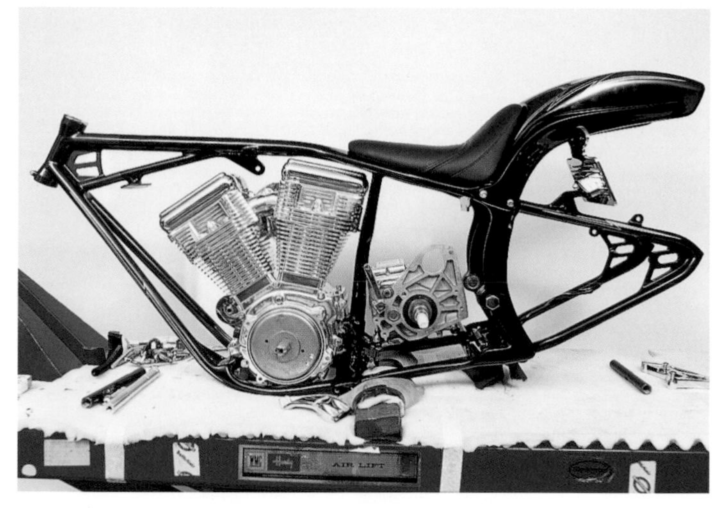

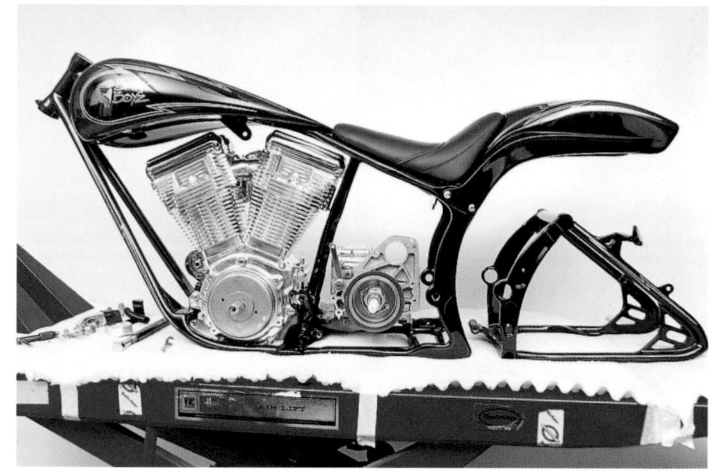

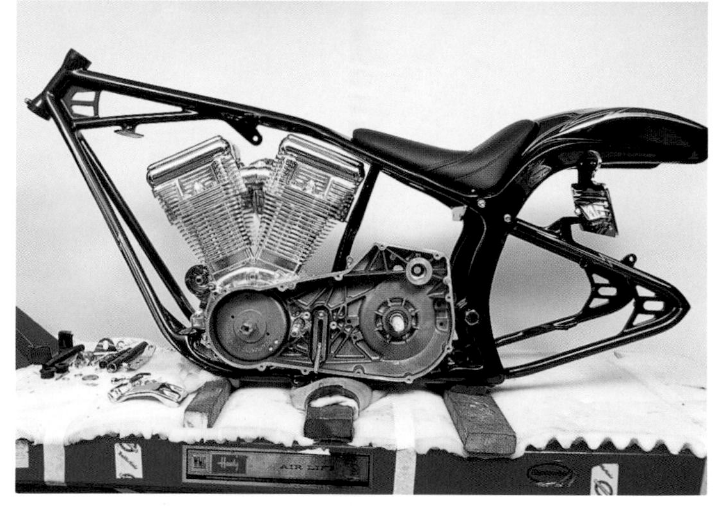

7 ABOVE: A close-up of the 1,450cc (88cu. in.) motor, showing the billet oil filter housing.

8 TOP RIGHT TO BOTTOM RIGHT:
Next the swing arm, license plate, and 1997 five-speed transmission.

9 The Battistinis custom aluminum gas tank has been fitted to check the mounting hardware, but will be removed shortly to ensure it doesn't get scratched during the build-up.

10 The inner case is fitted next. A chain primary drive will be used.

11 The seat has been removed and the Battistinis custom forks and Ness billet narrow-glide triple trees have been fitted. Note how the frame is strapped down onto foam to protect the paintwork. The process of wiring the bike has also begun.

12 A close look at the five-speed transmission shows the chromed "Progressive" shock absorbers underneath.

13 This is how professionally polished motors look — absolutely gorgeous!

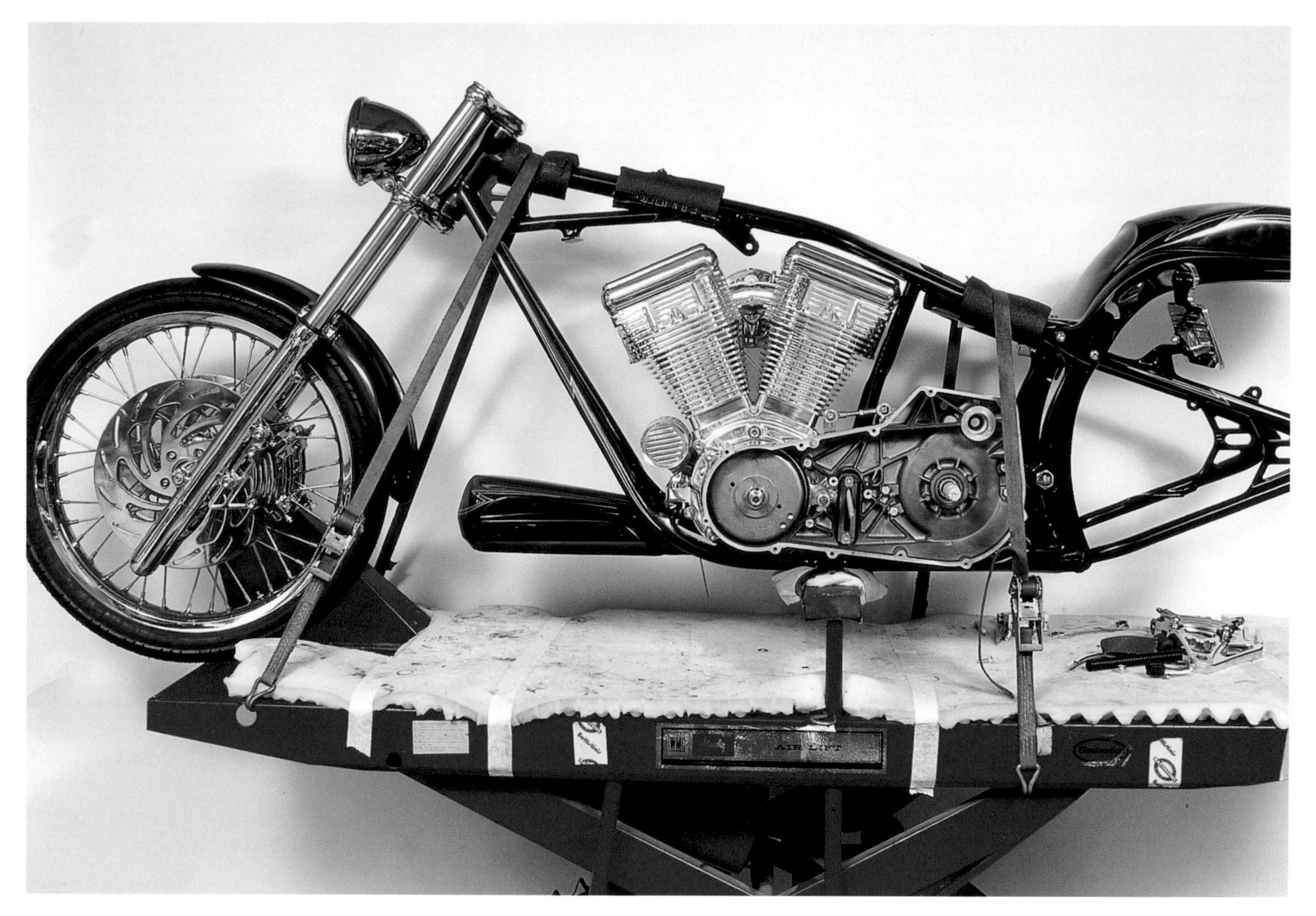

14 ABOVE: The front wheel and Battistinis fender have been added, as has the belly pan. The Akront rim is laced onto a chromed Ness hub.

15 LEFT: Close-up of the front wheel and brakes. The calipers are Ness items, gripping Ness "Smooth 7" rotors.

16 BELOW: Close-up of the mounting on the Ness headlight and triple trees.

17 ABOVE RIGHT: The front wheel is back out again, and a dry-fit of the outer primary case is underway to check the functioning of the gearshift mechanism. The importance of these dry-fit checks cannot be over-emphasized.

18 BELOW RIGHT: The gas tank and front wheel are back on, the primary is built, and the Battistinis custom handlebars fitted. Great care is again being taken to ensure no scratches occur — paper toweling is being used to stop the chain damaging the paint on the swing arm, and to stop the gas tank acquiring unwanted marks.

AIR LIFT
AIR LIFT

ARLEN NESS
Danny Gray
Battistinis

19 LEFT: Close-up of the Battistinis custom oil tank, the Ness fender struts, and the Danny Gray seat.

20 ABOVE: The handlebars have come off, but the back wheel is in place. If you want to build a bike this good, be prepared to keep fitting and removing parts until you are one hundred percent satisfied that everything is absolutely perfect.

21 And here's that rear wheel in close. Note that even at this range you still won't find a flaw or imperfection!

22 Now doesn't this powerplant look stunning? Again, look at how the lines of the components and paintwork all flow together. This sort of unity of design takes years to perfect, and is where art and engineering meet.

23 The Battistinis custom billet coil cover also blends in with the style of the rest of the bike.

24 The transmission cover is off in this picture, to facilitate checking the shift fork set-up.

25 ABOVE LEFT AND CENTER LEFT: The five-speed transmission has been completed, and the Ness exhaust is in place.

26

27 LEFT: Jeff McCann gas tank paint says it all . . .

28 ABOVE AND RIGHT: The bike is now finished and ready to leave its birthplace workbench.

29

30 And here's the man himself, Rikki Battistini.

BATT
Boyz

GRAHAM'S AMS BIKE

Graham Duffy conceived the overall concept of this bike to represent the popularity of wide-tired lowriders, but blended with the minimal bodywork of a muscle-bike. It utilizes the looks of a Softail, with the benefits of a rubber-mounted engine. It's a stunning example of his machining prowess, and does an excellent job of promoting his business, AMS Engineering, of Plymouth, England. It was completed in less than three months, including all the CAD design layouts. Graham took the bike to the Kent Custom Show — one of the most prestigious events in the UK — where it won "Best Engineering." No doubt this is just the first of many well-deserved trophies!

Graham is not in the business of making frames, so he was happy to sub-contract this work out. As he knew the look he wanted, all he had to do was find the right man for the job. That he found him can be seen in the pictures that follow.

THIS PAGE AND OPPOSITE: Graham's stunning bike is a testament to his bike building capabilities. Long, low and sleek, it has classic lines.

Owner....Graham Duffy, AMS
Model....Rubber Mount Softail
Builder....Owner
Build time....Three months
Engine....1997 Evo Big Twin, rebuilt by Surrey HD / Kev Drayton
Capacity....1,565cc (93cu. in.)
Crankcases....Delkron (polished)
Crank, Rods & Pistons....S&S
Cylinders....S&S Sidewinder (Hexed and polished)
Heads....Branch (Hexed and polished)
Cams....Andrews EV46
Lifters....HD
Ignition....Crane Hi-4
Engine covers(rocker, cam, pushrod)..Boyd's billet "Smooth"
Lifter blocks....Jim's Machining Billet
Rockers....Crane Rollers
Carburetor....S&S Super E (polished)
Air Cleaner....Boyd's Velocity Stack
Exhausts....Stainless steel one-offs by Planet Eng.
Mufflers....Billet end caps by AMS
Transmission....'97 FXR Revtech 5-Speed with Boyd's "Smooth" covers
Clutch and belt....Primo
Paintwork and moulding....Baz Allin at Pisces Paint
Polishing....AMS / Aquatech
Frame & swing arm....'97 Rubber Mount Softail by Planet Eng., 3-inch stretch, 38° rake
Shock absorbers....Fournales
Forks....Ceriani upside-down
Triple trees....AMS Wideglide
Wheels....AMS billet five-spoke, 19in x 3in front, 16in x 6.5in rear
Brakes....Performance Machine six-piston front, four-piston rear, GMA rotors
Gas tank and fenders....AMS hand-crafted aluminum
Handlebars....AMS / Aquatech
Forward controls....OMP / AMS
Seat....Racer Paul, Autotrim

Other special features:
AMS produced parts: Billet oil pressure gauge cover, top engine mount, twin coil mount, exhaust header clamps, lower twin pipe clamp, vented Derby cover, transmission inspection cover, speedo drive cover, billet transmission mounts, axle covers, chain adjuster covers, assorted hidden mounts on the frame, license plate frame, cable clamps, chainguard, stainless steel axles and spacers, inboard rear disc, billet sprocket and cush drive assembly.

Other parts: Landmark stainless steel engine stabilizers and gascap, Velva Ride front engine mount, Barnett braided throttle cable. Goodridge braided oil/fuel lines and fittings.

Let's follow the bike through its build-up:

1 ABOVE: This is what Graham started with; here the parts are at the Pisces Paint workshop waiting for the molding process to begin. The frame and swing arm were constructed by Planet Engineering, and feature a three-inch stretch.

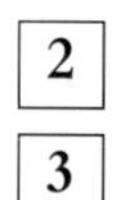

2 **3** Meanwhile Graham is collecting together all the little bits that he'll need when the build process starts. In these boxes are electrical parts such as switches, the horn, ignition coils, etc.

4 ABOVE: Here's the transmission carefully wrapped in cloth to protect it from scratches, dust etc. It's a 1997 Revtech FXR 5-Speed.

5 LEFT: The right side of the 1,565cc (93cu. in.) motor, with covers that will later be changed for some Boyd "Smooth Billet" items. The crank, rods, pistons and cylinders are all from S&S, and heads from Branch. The fins were hexed and polished before being fitted.

6 BELOW: And the left side. Note the Delkron logo on the crankcases; they're quality items which are very thick and strong.

Let's take a close look at the wheels which Graham made:

7 **8** ABOVE AND BELOW: The six and a half inch rear wheel; look for the valve stem — see it yet? This is the sort of attention to detail that shows the builder really cares. The stem is in fact integral with one of the rim bolts, and can be seen at the very top of the bolt circle. It carries an Avon 200/60 x 16 inch. Note that the GMA disc rotor is inboard of the rear sprocket. It's a wonderful example of Graham's expertise in the toolroom. The caliper is a Performance Machine four-pot.

9 RIGHT: At the other end Graham also made the front wheel and triple trees. They're fitted to a set of Ceriani upsidedown forks. The handlebars are one-offs by Aquatech/AMS.

Here we have the parts on return from Baz Allin's paintshop. Beautifully applied, the 2-pac Pearlescent Red paint shines as though wet.

10 LEFT: The front fender is a hand-crafted AMS aluminum item.

11 BELOW LEFT: As is the rear fender.

12 BELOW: The oil tank with some fittings installed. This was also made by Planet Engineering.

13 BOTTOM: The gas tank is a hand-crafted AMS aluminum item.

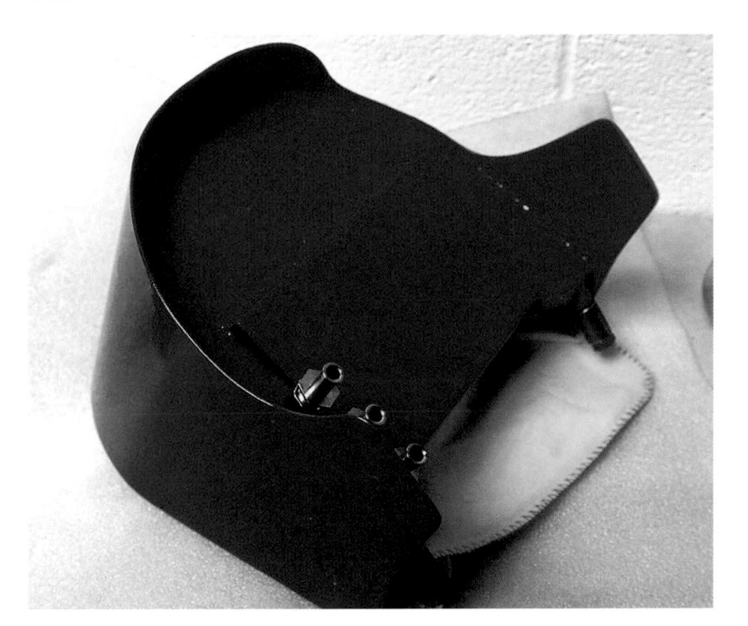

14 RIGHT: The frame. Graham has installed the lower triple tree to check the bearing installation. Note that he has wrapped the downtubes with bubblewrap to protect them from paint-chips by the tree. This is how professionals work.

15 CENTER RIGHT: A closer look at the top steering stem bearing.

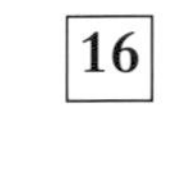
16 BELOW: Here Graham clears traces of paint from a bolt hole with a hand reamer. Note that he has also installed wires in the frame top tube to pull the harness through.

17 BOTTOM RIGHT: And here they can be seen exiting at the steering head. The knot is to stop them getting pulled through accidentally. In this shot the quality of the molding can be seen — or more to the point, it can't! That's what separates professional work from that of amateurs.

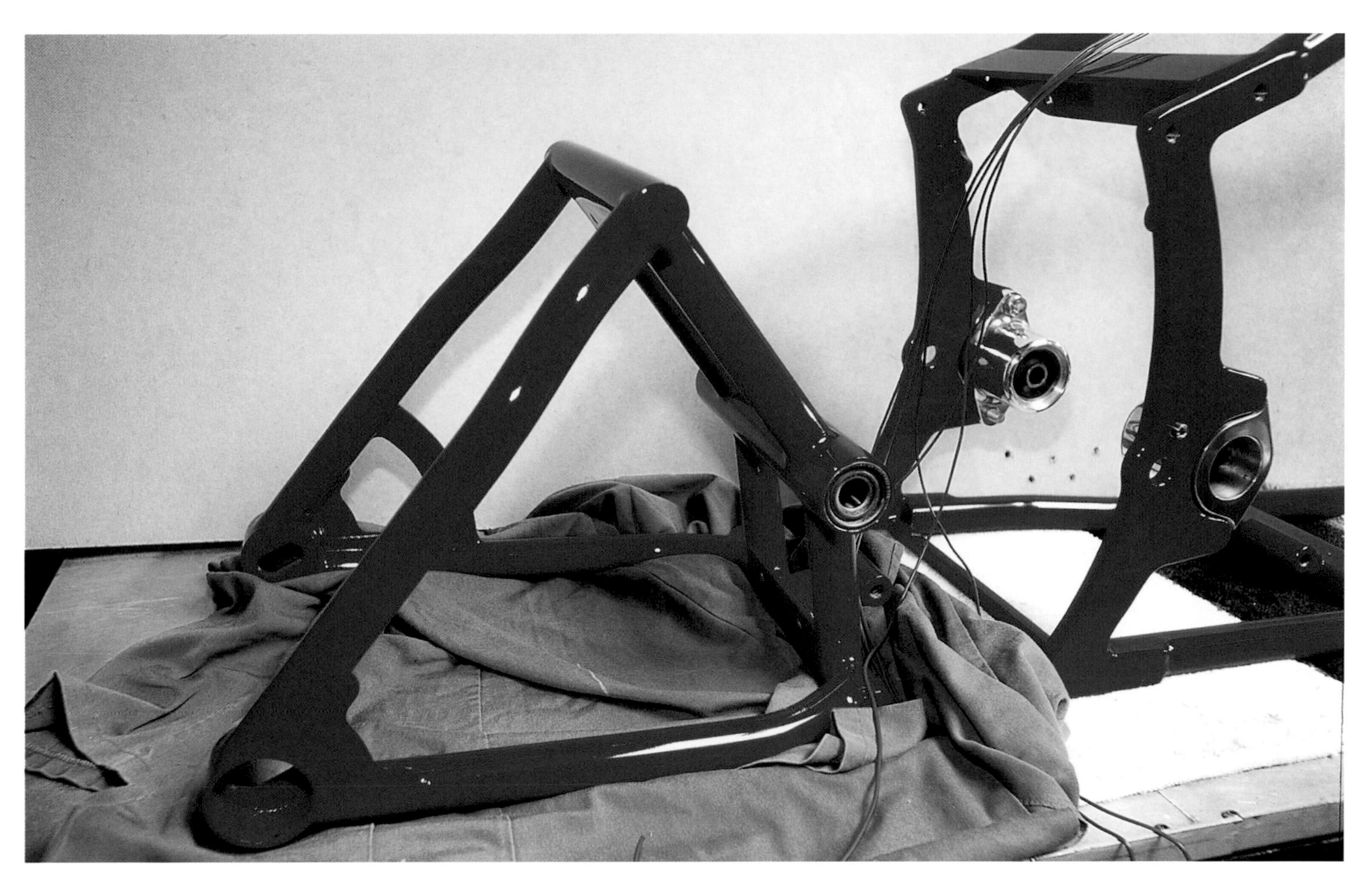

18 ABOVE: The swing arm ready for installation. Again, note the care with which the fresh paint is treated

19 BELOW: The frame is ready for all the detail parts to be fitted. Here some rubber grommets have been installed.

20 TOP: Some more parts ready for use — including the Aquatech/AMS headlight shell and the ignition coils.

21 ABOVE: Here's the Catseye tail light installed. It's a billet alloy unit which Graham made himself. Simple and elegant, it typifies the work on the entire bike.

22 **23** ABOVE AND LEFT: The bike is nearing completion now, with the motor and transmission installed. The rear wheel looks simply stunning in place.

24 RIGHT:
The rectifier/regulator unit in place. Again you can see there's a billet clamp which holds the clutch cable neatly against the frame downtube.

25 LEFT: The primary chaincase; inside is a Primo clutch and belt drive. Graham made the vented Derby cover.

26 BELOW: The handlebar layout again displays clean, elegant lines.

27 BOTTOM: The license plate mounting looks like a mirror from this angle. Look at how cleanly everything is installed. Work this good takes dedication and persistence.

28 RIGHT: The left-hand side of the motor.

29 BELOW RIGHT: The right-hand side of the motor.

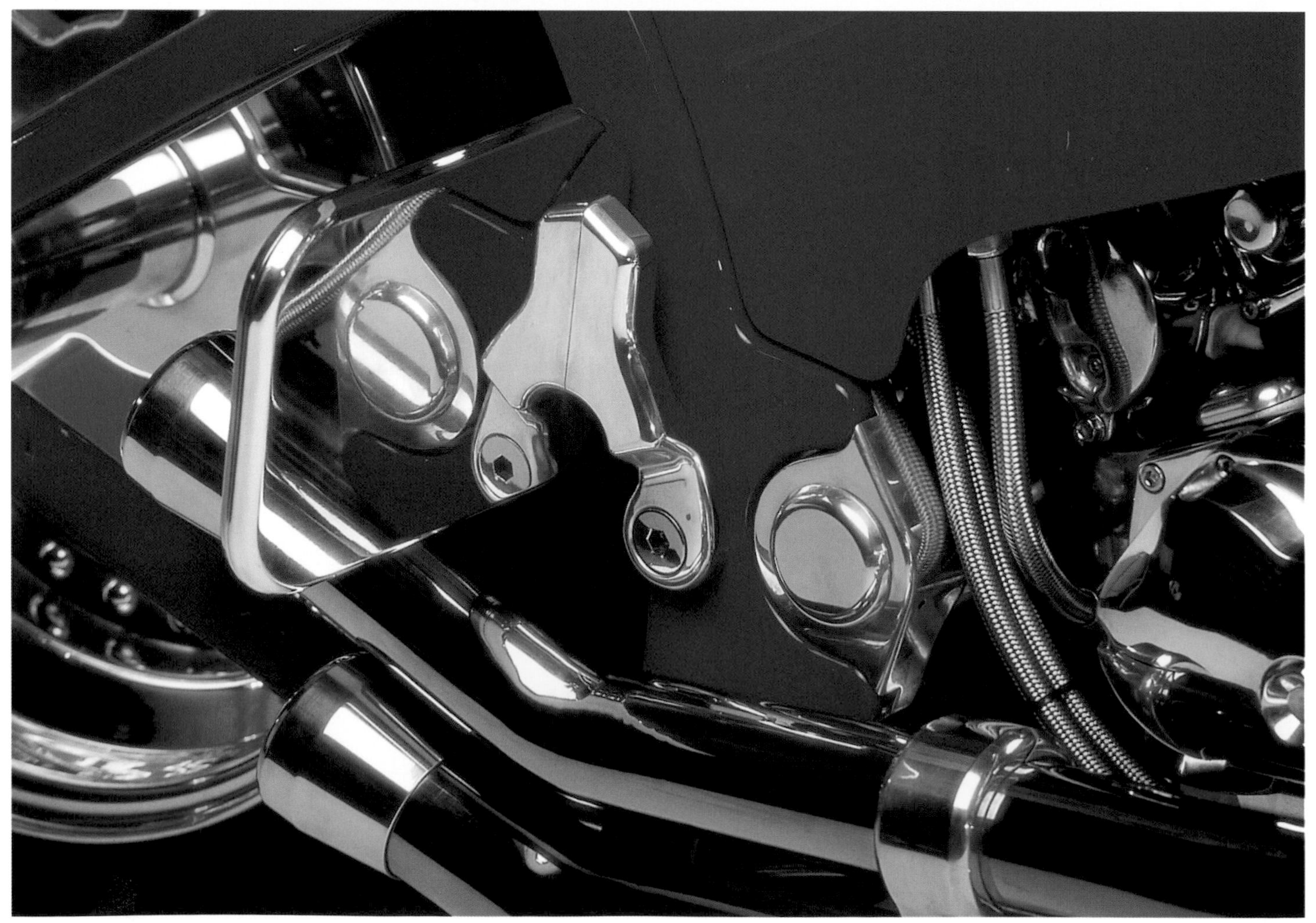

30 LEFT: The front end from the right-hand side.

31 BELOW: The rear wheel from the right-hand side.

32 ABOVE: The front end from the left-hand side.

33 BELOW: The rear wheel from the left-hand side.

34 BELOW RIGHT: And finally, the man himself, Graham Duffy.

STINGER

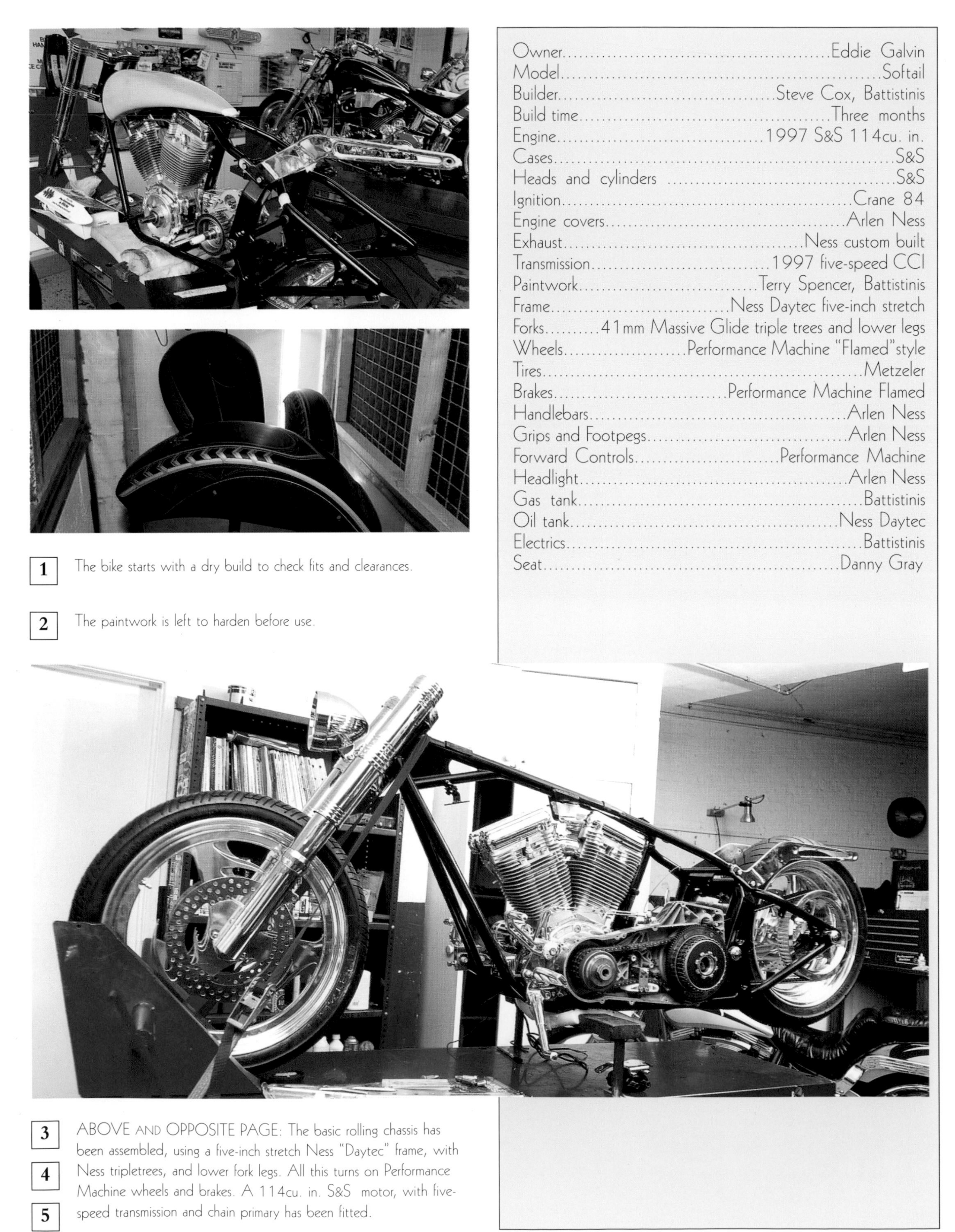

Owner	Eddie Galvin
Model	Softail
Builder	Steve Cox, Battistinis
Build time	Three months
Engine	1997 S&S 114cu. in.
Cases	S&S
Heads and cylinders	S&S
Ignition	Crane 84
Engine covers	Arlen Ness
Exhaust	Ness custom built
Transmission	1997 five-speed CCI
Paintwork	Terry Spencer, Battistinis
Frame	Ness Daytec five-inch stretch
Forks	41mm Massive Glide triple trees and lower legs
Wheels	Performance Machine "Flamed"style
Tires	Metzeler
Brakes	Performance Machine Flamed
Handlebars	Arlen Ness
Grips and Footpegs	Arlen Ness
Forward Controls	Performance Machine
Headlight	Arlen Ness
Gas tank	Battistinis
Oil tank	Ness Daytec
Electrics	Battistinis
Seat	Danny Gray

1 The bike starts with a dry build to check fits and clearances.

2 The paintwork is left to harden before use.

3 **4** **5** ABOVE AND OPPOSITE PAGE: The basic rolling chassis has been assembled, using a five-inch stretch Ness "Daytec" frame, with Ness tripletrees, and lower fork legs. All this turns on Performance Machine wheels and brakes. A 114cu. in. S&S motor, with five-speed transmission and chain primary has been fitted.

GREYHOUND EXPENSE-PAID TOUR
Mobilgas

HARLEY-DAVIDSON
CYCLES
SHELL
ARLEN NESS
Snap-on
METZELER
DUNLOP

TYPHOON
S&S
ARLEN
YAMAHA
METZELER
Edelbrock
WISECO
NOT ONLY AM I PERFEC
I RIDE A Harley TOO

6 **7** OPPOSITE: The big-inch S&S motor breathes through a Carl's Speed Shop "Typhoon 80" carburetor and velocity stack. The combination of polished motor and Ness covers looks stunning.

8 TOP: A close-up reveals the S&S logo on cases and cylinders.

9 ABOVE: The primary is installed and checked for clearances and alignment.

10 RIGHT: Steve Cox carefully installs the paintwork.

11 ABOVE: It's vital to check that the belt clears the tire. This is one of the drawbacks of fitting a wide rear tire — there's not much room for a chain, and even less for a belt. It can be a good idea to run some chalk against the side of the belt on both sides before the bike is ridden. If the chalk gets rubbed off, there's not enough clearance.

12 RIGHT: The wiring harness is now being constructed.

13 ABOVE: It's important to ensure that the battery fits properly. A trapped lead can set your bike on fire.

14 **15** RIGHT AND OPPOSITE: Ness Massive Glide triple trees in place on the finished bike.

16 Performance Machine "Flamed" wheels and brakes in close-up.

17

18 Fender struts are from Ness.

19 Oil pressure gauge and billet bracket are popular Ness items.

20 21 22

Here's that motor again.

The paint is of the standard that sets the true professionals apart . . . A bike to be proud of!

Stinger
Stinger

COUPÉ DE VILLE

Owner	Roger Winterburn, Windy Corner HD
Model	Softail
Builder	Rick James, Battistinis
Build time	Three months
Engine	1994 Evo 1,340cc (80cu. in.)
Cases	Stock
Cylinders	Edelbrock
Heads	Edelbrock
Engine covers	Ness "Radius Smooth"
Ignition	Dyna 2000
Exhaust	Ness Supertrap
Transmission	Polished 1994 five-speed
Paintwork	Terry Spencer, Battistinis
Frame	1997, Rick James modified, 5-inch stretch, 35° rake
Forks	41mm FLH with Battistinis billet caps
Triple trees	Ness Wide Glide
Wheels	Performance Machine Aero
Tires	Metzeler
Brake calipers	Performance Machine
Disc rotors	Performance Machine
Handlebars	Shortened Beach Bars
Handlebar grips and footpegs	Ness Twister
Fenders	Delcarlo
Lights	Ness
Gas tank	Battistinis
Oil tank	Modified stock
Electrics	Battistinis
Sprung seat	Chris Taylor

1 TOP: Here's where it all starts, with the 1,340cc (80cu. in.) motor. It features Edelbrock heads and cylinders, stock cases, and Ness covers. The transmission is a 1994 five-speed, with much polishing. Note the masking tape over the intake manifold to keep out unwanted airborne debris.

2 ABOVE: It takes hours of intensive polishing to get a transmission looking this good.

3 RIGHT: You can't rush the molding — it'll take far longer than you thought possible!

4 FAR RIGHT: Rick James gets his fingers busy applying the lightest possible touch of filler to get the molding just right.

5 BOTTOM RIGHT: The frame is now painted, and the motor installed. The wiring is underway. The primary is being assembled and the coil cover mounting is being checked.

Battistinis

6 The front end is now fitted, and the oil lines are being measured up and installed.

7 The gas tank is on and the wiring is undergoing its final checks. An S&S air cleaner is temporarily fitted for initial shakedown.

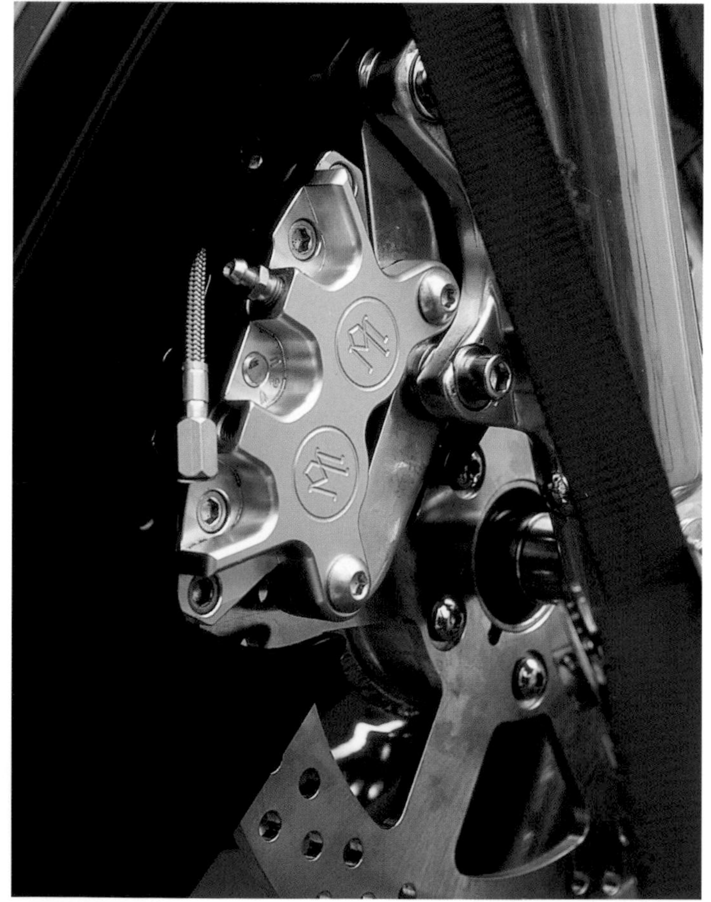

8 ABOVE: A close-up of the Performance Machine four-piston caliper.

9 ABOVE RIGHT: The bike is ready to come down to earth and make its way through its first few runs.

10 RIGHT: It has passed the shakedown tests, and the Ness "Radius Smooth" air cleaner is installed.

HARLEY DAVIDSON
Battistinis
AIR LIFT

Coupé De Ville

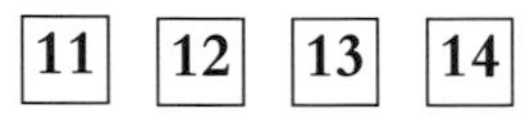

To build a bike this good needs care, skill, patience, and a lot of experience.

DYNA GLIDE

Here's another Battistinis' custom project. This time the brief was to take a stock Dyna Glide and turn it into a practical road bike without any radical alterations.

1 First, here's the pile of parts that have been removed.

2 LEFT: New shocks and swing arm have been fitted.

3 BELOW: Meanwhile the new headlight has been fitted, ready for the front end to go on.

4 ABOVE: New fork sliders, front wheel and brake rotor have replaced the original parts.

5 RIGHT: The bike is taking shape.

6 The air scoop is carefully installed.

7 ABOVE RIGHT AND RIGHT: The careful planning has paid off with the bike receiving the last few finishing touches, before coming off the workbench.

8

9 The completed bike displays the care and attention it has received during its meticulous build-up.

1 ABOVE AND BELOW: As you can see, there is nothing on this bike that doesn't absolutely, positively, have to be there! The bike is

2 very deliberately constructed in the most compact manner possible; the wheelbase is as short as the front exhaust will allow, and the transmission is fitted as close to the motor as the cases will permit — the oil pump had to be re-machined to clear the front of the tranny.

The affect of compacting all the heavy parts is to reduce what's known as the polar moment of inertia, which improves the steering response dramatically.

As many components as possible perform more than one function — for instance the frame is also the oil tank. In this picture the bike has road racing tires fitted; a slick rear, and an intermediate front. For different track conditions, there are also full wet weather racing tires.

The matched volume exhausts are hand made in seamless titanium, and are computer calculated for length. The transmission is a Quaife racing 4-speed wide-ratio unit. This helps minimize the number of gear-shifts (each of which cost valuable time!). The brake discs in this picture are cast iron road racing rotors, but when necessary, carbon fiber ones can be fitted.

The points cover is made from a high impact nylon — this is because the bike gets pushed to the limit on the track, which often results in crash damage. The use of this engineering material helps reduce the number of smashed timing covers.

SPIRIT OF SEMTEX

And finally, here's my own bike. It's very different from the others in this section, and perhaps could best be described as half way between a dirt track XR750 and a drag bike. It's built primarily for racing on English sprint hillclimb tracks, which are paved tracks around a mile long, which are often quite steep, and always have lots of tight turns.

The motor started out as a 1340 Evolution, but now measures 1,232cc. This is because the capacity limit for the class is 1,300cc. The bike is built for absolute performance — maximum acceleration, handling, and braking. This is achieved by having a fanatical obsession with weight; every component is made of the lightest material that will do the job. Therefore the wheels are magnesium, the frame is 7020 aircraft aluminum, and just about every nut and bolt is titanium.

I designed and made the frame myself, although the welding was done by Alan Welsh of Welbro Engineering — a true craftsman of the highest order.

First, let's take a look at the bike as it is now:

3 ABOVE RIGHT: The front exhaust is routed to give the tire as much clearance as possible . . .

4 RIGHT CENTER: The rear exhaust has to curve across to the left side of the bike to match the length of the front pipe. Matched lengths allow the cylinders to run more evenly, resulting in less vibration and more horsepower.

Owner	Patrick Hook
Fabrication by	Owner/Welbro Engineering
Engine	1232cc, short stroke, four-valve, (was an Evo Big Twin)
Builder	Owner
Cases	Delkron, modified
Crank	One-off S&S flywheels, modified and balanced by owner
Rods	S&S Supreme Duty, bored out to take Cosworth pins
Pistons	Cosworth 90mm Formula One race car, heavily modified
Cylinders	Stock, shortened, bored out, Beryllium Rings (no head gaskets)
Cam	Fueling four-valve
Carbs	2 x Weber IDF 40mm twin-throat racing, intakes by owner/Alan
Heads	four-valve fueling, modified
Ignition	Interspan racing system, no external power supply needed
Air Cleaners	Pancake type
Exhausts	Titanium, computer calculated length, matched front and rear
Silencers	Owner
Transmission	Quaife Racing 4-Speed wide-ratio
Clutch/Primary	Bob Newby Racing belt, alloy clutch and front pulley
Frame	1994, By owner/Welbro Engineering, 7020 Aluminum twin beam
Forks	Kayaba Upside Down Grand Prix
Rear shock	Kayaba Grand Prix, Titanium spring
Fasteners	Titanium, through drilled, safety wired
Overall weight	310lb!
Wheels	Marchesini Magnesium Grand Prix
Brakes	AP Racing Grand Prix Calipers/Carbon Fiber or Steel Rotors
Tires	Michelin Grand Prix, Wets, Intermediates or slicks
Size	130/17-inch front, 180/17-inch rear

5 LEFT: A low frontal area minimizes the aerodynamic drag, improving performance still further. Note the headstock has a clamp arrangement — there's an internal tube which carries the steering stem bearings; it's interchangeable with others for different steering rake angles, allowing fine tuning for different tracks. Notice also the amount of material machined out of the magnesium lower triple tree — you won't find a lighter item. Originally the top triple tree was also magnesium, but I destroyed it in a crash, so it's now aircraft aluminum. The steering damper is mounted below the triple tree. It's a Kayaba six-position adjustable grand prix racing item. It's mounted on spherical bearings, and allows the use of some extremely radical steering geometry.

6 LEFT: Here's where the serious horsepower is unleashed. Each of the two Weber IDF carburetors has two throats, and each of the four valve heads has two inlet ports; therefore the manifolds were constructed to give each valve its own independent system. This allows for super-fine tuning of the mixture, and a massive flow capability. It's particularly relevant because the usual practice of fitting one big carburetor drops the airspeed dramatically at anything other than maximum RPM. The fact that the intakes are downdraft is also very significant, as the normal sidedraft manifolds fitted to Harleys are a real performance restriction.

The downside is that at racing speeds it only does six miles to the gallon. Still, it's an improvement — at one time it was down to three!

The pipes entering the top of the gas tank are return lines from the fuel pump. The air cleaners are due to have some air scoops fitted into their top covers. This is to try and force feed the boxes for extra charge density. The decision was made to fit cleaners rather than the original trumpets because the front wheel was throwing small stones into the air, which on their return to earth were falling straight into the throttle bores — very bad for the motor!

7 BELOW LEFT: Here we can see the ignition box, made by Interspan. It's a self contained high energy unit, which can be triggered by points or by electronic pick-ups. It will run for about 45 minutes before it needs recharging from an external battery. There is also a full plasma ignition system made by Interspan, but I haven't raced with it yet.

Below the ignition is the $1\frac{5}{8}$-inch belt primary, which comprises an alloy clutch drum and front pulley, made by Bob Newby Racing.

There is no compensating mechanism, so the whole thing can be run close into the motor, minimizing overhang, and reducing the load on the crank and transmission bearings. The bike is fired up by an external system driven by a 24V truck starter motor. It engages with the front pulley nut, hence the lock bolt.

8 LEFT: The rear shock absorber is a Kayaba Grand Prix unit. It features adjustable high and low speed compression and rebound damping, as well as spring preload, and with different springs the rate can also be altered. The spring is made of titanium. The swing arm subframe has spherical jointed linkages, so the lever ratio of the rear geometry is variable; its length is also adjustable for ride height adjustment independent of the suspension settings.

The chain is made for racing, hence it's very narrow, and very light. The rear sprocket is also thin and light. It's held on by light-weight titanium bolts, and the rear axle is a hollow grand prix item.

9 ABOVE: A close look at the front end reveals AP Racing calipers, braided steel lines, titanium banjo bolts, and massive floating rotors. The wheel is a 17-inch magnesium Marchesini unit. Note that all the fasteners are hollow titanium.

10 ABOVE RIGHT: The oil tank sight glass is clearly visible on the frame spar. The frame is made from a triple box extrusion, and holds four pints of synthetic racing oil. The motor is a high rpm short-stroker with light flywheels; four valve cylinder heads are by Fueling Engineering.

11 RIGHT: The right-hand footrest plate also acts as the locking mechanism for the swing arm axle nut.

12 When the bike was first built, the carburetors had no air cleaners, instead they had intake trumpets. Here the bike is still under construction. You can see that the fuel tank is unpolished, and is awaiting welding of the fuel return line fittings. The area forward of the carbs carries the fuel pump and its battery. (Photo by K. Solomon.)

13 Here the system is complete and working well. (Photo by K. Solomon.)

14 LEFT: But here the system is no longer working, as I've crashed it again. (Photo by Dr. P. Travers.)

15 ABOVE: Here, during a dry build of the bike, the twin plasma ignition boxes are being checked for fit. The transmission case positioning is also being examined. It's important to check and recheck everything at this stage. (Photo by K. Solomon.)

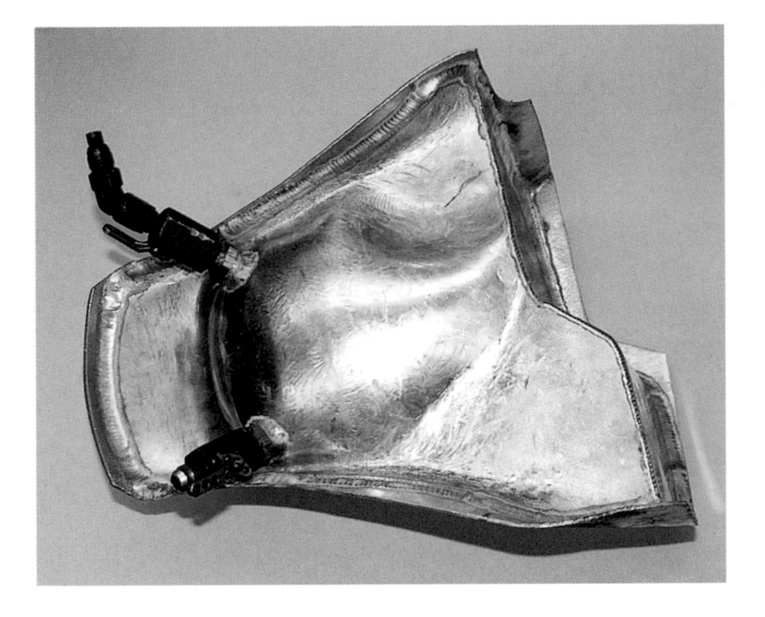

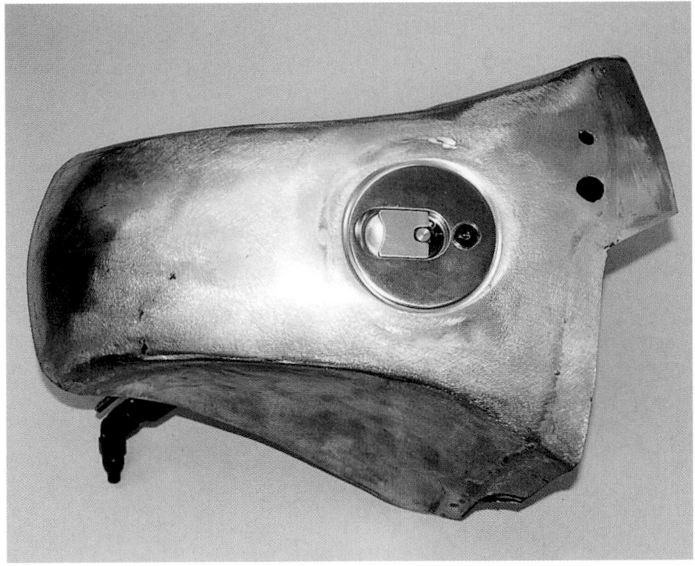

16 **17** ABOVE and ABOVE RIGHT: The underside of the gas tank shows the clearancing necessary to fit over the rear cylinder head and around the carburetors. The gas taps are high flow aircraft items. The filler cap is a flush fitting racing unit. (Photo by K. Solomon.)

18 BELOW: In this picture the fit of the fuel pump cover and the front fender mounts are being perfected. (Photo by K. Solomon.)

19 Getting the chain alignment right is critical to building a successful bike, so at this stage it's being finalized. Once this is done, the alignment of the primary transmission pulleys can be checked. (Photo by K. Solomon.)

Now is a good time to double check the clearance of the rear tire with the suspension fully compressed. Things to examine on a road bike are the wires to the rear light, and any bolts for the rear fender and seat mountings. If you have an exhaust similar to mine, then you need to check this too.

20 People are forever asking me what the bike goes like, so here I'm about to show them — first I warm the center of the tire with a burnout.

21 Then I lean the bike over to get the sides hot as well.

22 The light goes green, I'm leaning over the front as far as I can get, and the rear is spinning.

23 Even with my weight over the front, and with the rear spinning, it's still nigh on impossible to keep the wheel down!

24 Returning to the pits after a successful run, and a look of surprise, "Wow — I didn't crash it!"

25 And this is me — no, you won't see me smiling early on race day!

FINISHED EXAMPLES

FAT BOY

These two Fatboys were built by Battistinis to demonstrate that stunning customs could be achieved using only parts straight from the Ness and Performance Machine catalogs. Both were stock new bikes when the project was started — the results speak for themselves, although what is remarkable is how subtle the differences are.

TRIKE

ABOVE and RIGHT: This clean Shovel trike shows that customs can look good and be practical for everyday use. Note the tweek bar on the forks to increase the stiffness of the front end — this helps the steering, particularly under braking. The motor is breathing through an S&S carburetor and air cleaner. The link pipe between the exhausts helps the balance of the cylinders, especially at low rpm. The tool-roll under the headlight is a good idea — you never know when a bolt is going to work loose, especially on a riding partner's bike!

FLAMES

ABOVE and LEFT: This beautiful Shovel chop epitomizes the stretched front end look — long, long forks, small discs, multi-spoke wheel, and clean "slab" triple trees. The continuity of the bike's style is carried through nicely with the sleek straight pipes, the low seat, and clean handlebar control layout. The flames are nice too.

MORE FLAMES

ABOVE and RIGHT: There are high 'bars, and there are HIGH 'bars! The short front end accentuates their height — in many places they would be illegal. The Evo motor shows nicely what can be done by highlighting the edges of the cylinder fins against black engine paint. The crisp edges to the flames help to continue this theme throughout the bike.

RED BIKE

ABOVE and LEFT: In contrast to the "long and sleek" look, there's the "long but solid" look, which this bike carries off beautifully. The big-bore high-level exhaust system helps in this respect, as does the massive triple tree/front fork combination. The braided stainless steel line to the transmission cover is for the hydraulic clutch. The painted S&S air cleaner is a nice touch, as is the oil cooler on the front downtubes.

SMOOTHNESS

ABOVE: Here's another classic Arlen Ness creation. It utilizes the concept of flowing bodywork with a rubber-mounted engine to form a bike worthy of its name — "Smooth" it is! The impressive all-aluminum bodywork was by Craig Naff, and the 1,340cc (80cu. in.) motor was built by Ness, mostly from S&S parts.

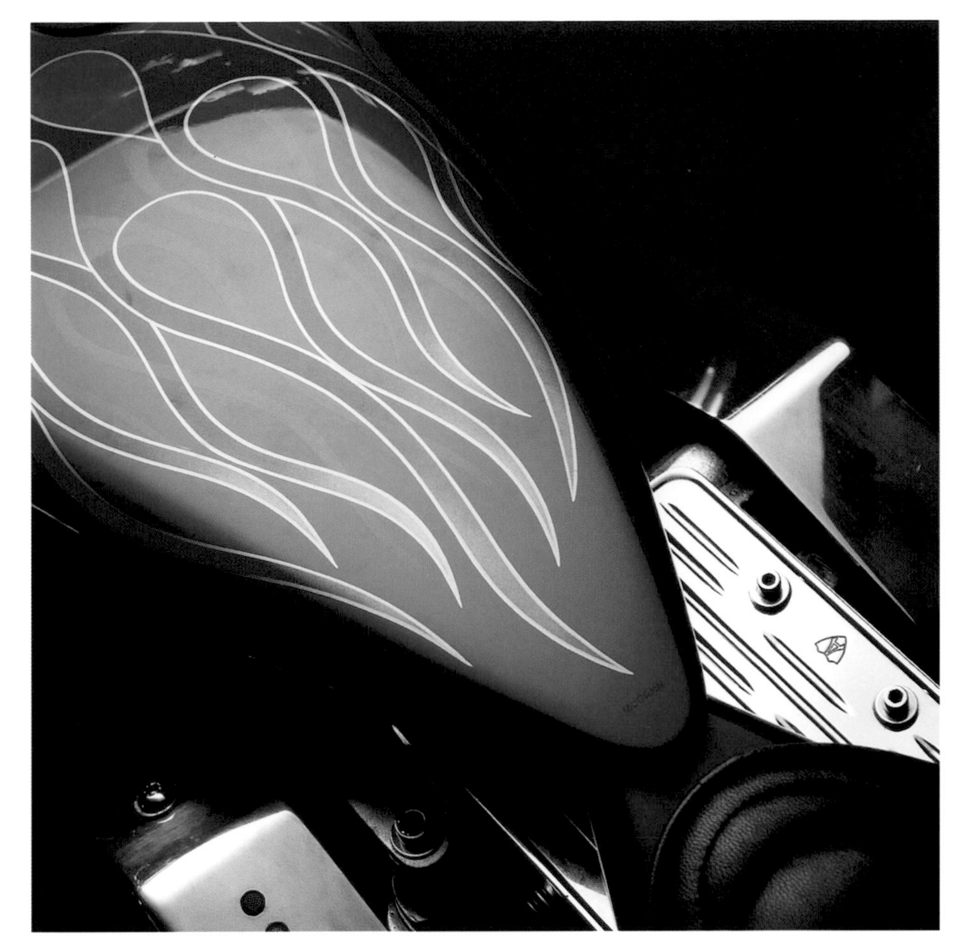

CRUISER

LEFT and BELOW: This Softail Rubbermount was built by Jeff Duval of Battistinis as the ultimate in muscle-engined customs — the motor is a full 2,050cc (125cu. in.) of raw power! The super-strong four-cam billet cases are from Delkron — giving pushrod geometry far superior to the standard Big Twin set-up. The idea behind the bike's construction was as a rolling test-bed for the Cruiser line of products. Look out for this bike at the stoplights!

RED SHIFT

ABOVE and BELOW: This 89cu. in. FXST is another by Battistinis. The motor features Carl's Speed Shop heads and cam, with an S&S crank, rods, and pistons. The modified Softail frame has a Battistinis gas tank and Ness fenders; the paint was by Jeff McCann — the color is described as "Red, Red and Red!"

PASADENA

ABOVE and TOP: When Jeff Duval built this machine, he based it on a Dyna Low Rider. It took him eight months to complete using a stock capacity motor topped with Patrick billet heads and an S&S carb. The frame is stretched five inches and raked out to 40 degrees; the wheels are Performance Machine Twisters with matching discs.

BACKFIRE

ABOVE and BELOW: Rikki Battistini only took two months to complete this Softail Chopper — the frame is a Ness Daytec, with 29 degrees of rake and two inches of stretch. The lower end of the motor is mostly S&S, with the top end finished off with Edelbrock heads. As with most customs to come out of the Battistinis' workshop, Rikki used a quality seat from Danny Gray.

WARBIRD

ABOVE and LEFT: If you thought that the two months it took to create "Backfire" was quick, this FXR only took Battistinis four weeks to build! The frame was left alone other than to have detail molding applied under the Terry Spencer paint. The stock capacity motor has Edelbrock Performer heads, S&S cases, and a Crane Fireball cam. The pipes are by Supertrapp, and the air-cleaner is a Ness Airscoop mounted on an S&S Super E carburetor.

SMOOFTALE

THIS PAGE: When Arlen Ness built "Smoothness" he made two identical frames; this is the second one, which Jeff Duval acquired and spent eight months working on to build the custom you see here. The paint is another Jeff McCann job in Cadillac Candy Red over molding by Terry Spencer. The seat on this bike is by Dave Batchelor, mounted next to an aluminum gas tank made by Battistinis, as were the custom exhausts which set the bike off nicely.

BIKE X

ABOVE and LEFT: This Softail with eye-catching Yellow/Pearl White paint by Terry Spencer has 35 degrees of rake and five inches of stretch in the Battistinis frame. The swing arm is by Boyds, suspended with Progressive shock absorbers. The front end features Ness Massive Glide forks, shortened by one inch. The bike rolls on Performance Machine Phantom wheels with matching discs.

ABOVE, ABOVE RIGHT, and BELOW: This stunning example of an Evo trike was built by Nottingham Custom Cycles. Owner Dave Stewart lost a leg in a collision some time ago, but refused to give up riding, so had the machine you see here built to his specific wants and needs. The motor has plenty of billet engine covers in evidence, along with RevTech heads, drawing through a Carl's Speed Shop Typhoon carburetor. The tough look of this trike is helped by the Jaguar independent rear axle, adding to the "no messing" appeal of it all.

FAT TRACKER

ABOVE and BELOW: This bike shows that a tastefully executed custom doesn't need to have a radical frame or a monster capacity to show class. The motor is mostly stock, with the addition of a Crane cam and ignition, matched with an S&S carb to liven it up. The rocker covers are by Ness, as are the lifter blocks, the primary cover, cam cover, pushrod covers, etc. The wheels are by Performance Machine — Laser style.

FXRSS

ICE COOL

ABOVE LEFT and LEFT: Here's another bike built by Jeff Duval, this time with the assistance of Steve Cox. As you might guess from its name, it's based on an FXR. It has a Battistinis/Cobra frame that's been stretched by five inches and also kicked out to 40 degrees. The Carl's Speed Shop motor has been opened up to 1,440cc (88cu. in.) courtesy of their own heads, with Axtell pistons attached to crank, rods, and cases by S&S. The forks were prototypes made in conjunction with Graham Duffy (whose AMS bike is featured in the "step-by-step" section). The clean look of the front end is enhanced by a wheel laced up with stainless steel spokes on a Ness hub and an Akront rim.

ABOVE: Finally we have a long, sleek Battistinis custom to show that, no matter how many bikes you build, you can always vary the theme enough to stamp a mark of individuality throughout. Compare for instance the front end with that of "FXRSS" — even though they both use a spoked wheel with similar rake and frame stretch, they've turned out totally different. When you set out to build your custom, learn from the professionals — plan ahead, think it through, and take the time to get it right!

INDEX